Mutual
TREASURE

*Published in association with the
Center for Christian Studies, Gordon College*

Mutual
TREASURE

Seeking Better Ways for Christians and Culture to Converse

Edited by
Harold Heie & Michael A. King

Foreword by
Richard Mouw

Cascadia

Publishing House
Telford, Pennsylvania

copublished with
Herald Press
Scottdale, Pennsylvania

Cascadia Publishing House LLC orders, information, reprint permissions:
contact@cascadiapublishinghouse.com
1-215-723-9125
126 Klingerman Road, Telford PA 18969
www.CascadiaPublishingHouse.com

Mutual Treasure
Copyright © 2009 by Cascadia Publishing House
a division of Cascadia Publishing House LLC, Telford, PA 18969
All rights reserved.
Copublished with Herald Press, Scottdale, PA
Library of Congress Catalog Number: 2009006831
ISBN 13: 978-1-931038-57-7; ISBN 10: 1-931038-57-0
Book design by Cascadia Publishing House
Cover design by Dawn Ranck

Library of Congress Cataloguing-in-Publication Data
Mutual treasure : seeking better ways for Christians and culture to converse / edited by Harold Heie and Michael A. King ; foreword by Richard
Mouw.
    p. cm.
Includes bibliographical references.
    Summary: "Rejecting both Christian withdrawal from and confrontational approaches to culture, this book calls for engaging others by coming
alongside them, building relationships of trust through which to seek mutual treasure"--Provided by publisher.
    ISBN-13: 978-1-931038-57-7 (trade pbk. : alk. paper)
    ISBN-10: 1-931038-57-0 (trade pbk. : alk. paper)
    1. Christianity and culture. 2. Dialogue--Religious aspects--Christianity.
I. Heie, Harold, 1935- II. King, Michael A., 1954- III. Title.

BR115.C8M2167 2009
261'.1--dc22

2009006831

16 15 13 12 11 10 09   10 9 8 7 6 5 4 3 2

For now we see in a mirror, dimly, but then we will see face to face. Now I know only in part; then I will know fully, even as I have been fully known.
—1 Corinthians 13:12

CONTENTS

Dr. Stephen V. Monsma, Henry Institute, Calvin College

"Under the dialogue model, one starts with trust and respect, moves to an understanding of what motivations and perspectives underlie the differing positions, and from there finds areas of common ground and larger areas of agreement."

Monsma argues that Christians are called to be agents for God's redemptive purposes in today's predominantly secular culture, thereby rejecting the option of withdrawing from culture. But, he rejects a confrontational approach to engagement with culture, except under extraordinary circumstances. Instead, he proposes a dialogue model that starts with getting to know the persons who disagree with you.

Dr. James Waller, Auschwitz Institute
for Peace and Reconciliation

"Engagement with ideas in the secular academy is, of necessity, engagement with others (real people) who carry those ideas. In that engagement, I try to practice (not always successfully) a

relational humility that leaves open spaces for me, and others, to tear down the barriers of 'us' and 'them' that, too often, hinder effective engagement."

Waller has proposed a theory as to "why ordinary people sometimes do extraordinary evil" that is deeply informed by his Christian faith perspective. He reports that his theory has gained a respectful hearing within an elite group of mostly secular Holocaust and Genocide scholars, largely because he has sought to exemplify intellectual, worldview, and relational humility in his personal engagement with these scholars.

Dr. Paul DeWeese, former member,
Michigan House of Representatives

"I frequently worked alongside African-American clergy in Lansing. . . . I made a commitment to listen, to understand their perspectives on the issues that were important to their communities. As I listened, I came to understand better the ways in which I benefited from 'white privilege.'"

Appalled by the influence of special interest groups and the hyper-partisanship of contemporary politics, DeWeese sought to exemplify a "personalism in politics," which included seeking common ground with members of the opposing party concerning legislative initiatives that would foster basic human dignity. He found that getting to know members of the other party on a personal level helped him to build bridges across both racial and partisan divides.

Dr. Susan Emmerich, CEO,
Emmerich Environmental Consulting

"The conflict stemmed from the differences in worldview and language between the two groups. . . . The two groups talked past each other, each not listening to or understanding the other,

or sometimes not respecting their neighbor's worldview. . . . [A broader view of 'neighbor'] led to individual Tangiermen asking forgiveness from CBF (Chesapeake Bay Foundation) staff for ostracizing them and to CBF staff asking for forgiveness for their mistakes."

In contrast to the detached approach of the scientists who addressed the environmental problems in Chesapeake Bay, Emmerich moved in with families of the watermen of Tangiers Island who fished the Bay. By getting to know them personally, she slowly developed the trust needed to dialogue with them and invite them to address the environmental problems they were partly responsible for creating.

CHAPTER 5 • 93
ROUNDTABLE CONVERSATION: HOSPITALITY IN THE ACADEMY
Rev. David Thom, faculty ministry at Harvard and MIT

"Persons in our college and university communities who do not share our Christian faith commitment do not typically flock to the lectures on the Christian message that we sponsor. We then too easily console ourselves with the mistaken notion that when Christian thought has been made available in the written word or through open-invitation lectures that our work as Christians is done."

In his case study, Dave Thom describes bringing together hundreds of scholars, about fifty at a time, where Christian scholars are outnumbered by non-Christian scholars, for evenings of dinner and dialogue among faculty at Harvard and MIT and in the Amherst-based Five-College area. Roundtables have met more than thirty times to explore the intersection of contemporary academic thought and Christian thought on issues related to science, art, and religion. Here Thom describes the origins of The Roundtable and assesses their accomplishments.

CHAPTER 6 • 110
CHANGING THE CULTURE, ONE FILM AT A TIME
Mr. Jack Hafer, Independent Film Maker

"The content, tone, and style of the film can build a mutual trust between filmmakers who are mutually involved in the Great Conversation. . . . I make films that I think deal with the

human condition and thereby invite people of all persuasions to find themselves in them in some way."

By describing two of his film projects, the feature film *To End All Wars* and the documentary *Wall of Separation*, Hafer illustrates how he attempts to influence the secular culture by using film as a means for dialogue with that culture. He also relates the challenges of operating in the highly secular film culture and how he has worked to overcome those challenges.

CHAPTER 7 • 125
TO KNOW AND BE KNOWN:
EVANGELICALS AND INTERFAITH DIALOGUE
Dr. Marvin Wilson, Gordon College

"If agreement on everything is a necessity for dialogue, then there can be no dialogue. The main prerequisite for dialogue is to come to the table with the right to self-definition, and to grant that same right to others around the table. . . . Dialogue will not work if we must be 'right' on every issue. We have to listen in relation to every issue—and listen with a teachable spirit. . . . If the sole purpose of talking is to get an 'opponent' to concede rather than to see and understand another perspective, then we are not engaging in dialogue.

Appalled by the high degree of ignorance, misconceptions, suspicion and mistrust that existed between the Jewish and Evangelical Christian communities, Wilson has devoted over forty-five years to building bridges between these two faith communities by means of a dialogue that avoids stereotypes and demonization and seeks greater mutual understanding and learning from one another. After describing the dynamics of this career-long process, he argues for the need to further expand the conversation into a "trialogue" that will engage Muslim perspectives.

CHAPTER 8 • 144
CONVERSATIONS ON HOMOSEXUALITY AS A
QUEST TO LOVE ENEMY PREJUDICES
Dr. Michael A. King, President, Cascadia Publishing House LLC

"I have come to summarize genuine conversation as involving a mutual quest for treasure in our own and the other's viewpoint.

*. . . The first move is 'to make as clear as I can why I hold this
position (prejudice) and why you might find in it treasure to
value in your own quest for truth.' The second key move is to
grow in my own understandings by incorporating as much of
the other's perspective as I can without losing the integrity of
my own convictions.'"*

Drawing on a model of "genuine conversation" inspired by
Hans Georg-Gadamer, King reports on his experiences orchestrating conversations about homosexuality within the
Mennonite Christian community, and beyond, and evalu-
ates what happens when the quest is not for victory but for
mutual learning. By noting both successes and failures, he
highlights the potentialities and well as the limits of nurtur-
ing genuine conversation, especially when dealing with issues as controversial as that of homosexuality.

CHAPTER 9 • 161
FINDING LIGHT IN BROKEN HOPE:
AN ALTERNATIVE TO ADVERSARIAL CRIMINAL JUSTICE

Ms. Tammy Krause, Outreach Specialist,
Federal Public Defender

*"I spent the majority of the lunch meeting answering the fami-
lies' questions and listening to their skepticism and concerns. At
times such as this, it is important to listen to the apprehension
without an answer or argument. People need to be heard and to
feel valued for what they have to say. . . . When you journey
alongside persons faithfully and witness their dark moments of
pain and suffering, there will be a time that you will find yourself present as they find their voices, as they sing the song which
never stops, and you know you are in a very holy place."*

Drawing on principles of restorative justice, Krause describes her arduous attempts to enable the families of victims in capital murder cases to gain a voice in the legal proceedings. Focusing on developing trust in an adversarial
system characterized primarily by mistrust, she cites a case
example to illustrate how honesty, integrity, trust, and respect can change the judicial course for those most deeply
impacted in capital cases.

The Foreword

Recently I heard a speaker issue yet another impassioned call for Christians to "engage culture." Part of me takes some comfort in such pleas. This particular speaker had the zeal of a convert, coming from a part of the evangelical world in which such calls to engagement are a rather recent phenomenon. Like many other evangelicals, he was enthusiastic about what were for him some rather new theological discoveries: "the cultural mandate," Christ's lordship over all of life, the importance of a comprehensive "biblical worldview." These are laudable discoveries.

But I also get a little nervous about generic calls to cultural engagement. There are different ways of getting engaged. One obvious way is when a couple goes public with a loving commitment to each other. Another is when a military unit engages an enemy force. Too often Christian calls for cultural engagement are more like the military version than the courtship variety. We are told that we have let "the world" take over the culture, and we need to get out there and take it back. The call to engagement, then, comes across as a recruiting effort for cultural warriors.

Not that the courtship model is the proper alternative. The ravages of our shared human fallenness are all too obvious in the various spheres of cultural interaction. We have to be careful that we do not fall in love with that which is displeasing to God. Our shared fallenness is much too obvious in our various spheres of cultural interaction.

Fortunately there are several points on the engagement spectrum between military campaigns and preparation for marriage, and this excellent book of essays has located exactly the right point: *friendship*. To be a friend is to come alongside of the other person. It is to make room in one's own consciousness for the other person's hopes and fears. To be a friend is to be committed to an ongoing dialogue, a process of genuine listening and empathetic responding.

The writers of these essays have made a commitment to that dialogic—that friendship—process in engaging the larger culture. They are rightly disillusioned with the kind of confrontational approach that demonizes those with whom we see ourselves as being in disagreement on important matters. Calling for a different spirit, the writers have provided us with helpful overviews and guidelines for cultural engagement, as well as stimulating explorations of what it means to pursue that engagement in specific cultural arenas: politics, the environment, film, the academy, sexual relations, courts of law, interreligious encounters, and the like.

In all of this, the writers of these essays not only model an appropriate spirit of cultural engagement. They also teach us some important things about the specific areas they address. Even more important, they teach us what it can be like to learn from others—including people with whom we disagree on some basic issues of life. Properly understood, cultural engagement is not simply having an *impact on* culture, it is also being *changed by* engaging the complexities we encounter there. A friendly cultural engagement can be a way of growing in the Christ who is the lord over all spheres of cultural life. This book of essays is a rich gift to those of us who are committed to experiencing that kind of Christian growth.

—*Richard J. Mouw*
  President and Professor of Christian Philosophy
  Fuller Theological Seminary

EDITORS' PREFACE

We are appalled at the confrontational nature of much public discourse. Persons having diametrically opposed views on an important issue typically argue from fixed positions. There is no intention to budge: "I have the truth, you don't, listen up." The only purpose of engagement is to demolish the other's point of view.

Christians are not immune from this prevailing culture of confrontation. Those Christians who get air time on TV and radio often relish the battle. There are, however, Christians who get little or no air time who are committed to a better way. They are the heroes of this book, which features their stories.

A premise underlying this better way is that it is easier to talk about disagreements with friends than with strangers. We often experience this in private life. We dare to propose its extension to public discourse.

This better way starts with building relationships of mutual trust with those with whom you disagree, getting to know them well enough to understand their points of view and why they hold their positions. You then talk respectfully about your differences in the spirit of being open to finding some "treasures" in their contrary positions, hoping that they will likewise find some treasures in your point of view.

This dialogic model sounds laughable in our brutish world. How much more naïve can we get? Nevertheless, we have found Christian scholars and practitioners in a wide variety of fields who have exemplified this model, as their stories will reveal. Motivated by a common belief that Christians are called to be agents for God's redemptive purposes, they have rejected the strategy of being confrontational agents, embracing, rather, the strategy of "coming alongside" those they wish to serve.

And they have found that it works. Coming alongside others has opened doors for them to exert a significant redemptive influence in their respective spheres of activity. But they don't use a dialogic strategy because it works. They engage others in this better way because it is the right thing for Christians to do. It is a deep expression of that love for others to which Jesus Christ has called them. The fact that it works is a nice bonus.

We hope and pray for the seeds sown by these stories to lead to the fruitful harvest we at least glimpse in our wilder dreams. We hope there is inspiration in the very fact that this book exists as a collaboration between an evangelical Christian editor and sponsoring organization (Center for Christian Studies) and an Anabaptist Christian editor and press (Cascadia) whose traditions do not always see eye to eye yet who beyond differences spy treasure in each other's viewpoints.

We hope we model some of what we preach by the very fact that both of us as editors sometimes find ourselves in creative tension with core assumptions held by chapter writers. Obviously, for example, an Anabaptist editor would not always approach from an evangelical perspective the question of how Christians best engage culture. Nor would an evangelical editor necessarily want to be forced into developing a primarily Anabaptist book. Yet in this book, neither of us sees our main concern as being whether we agree with a given writer (of whatever tradition) or even a given approach to seeking better ways to converse with culture. Our concern is not whether given assumptions are always exactly right but to offer examples of how different ones of us, from a range of backgrounds, may illustrate a pursuit of mutual treasure.

As you consider the opportunities that you have to engage others in your sphere of activity, we encourage you to test and even, if the fruits you experience turn out to justify it, to embrace the various quests for a dialogic model of discourse this book shares.

—*Harold Heie, Orange City, Iowa*
  Michael A. King, Telford, Pennsylvania

ACKNOWLEDGMENTS

We could never have predicted the end from the beginning. We started with three case study events sponsored by the Center for Christian Studies at Gordon College (Mass.). Titled *Christians Engaging Culture: Models for Public Policy Practitioners, Politicians, and Scholars,* the project featured three of our essayists. It was while processing the various response papers for these three events that we decided to expand the number of case studies in our projected book. Alas, space limitations then precluded the possibility of publishing some excellent response papers. However, we now wish to acknowledge those many scholars who contributed to the success of these events.

In November 2004, Susan Drake Emmerich was the featured speaker at the first case study event hosted at Gordon College, presenting an earlier version of the essay included in this volume. This event was convened by Steve Bouma-Prediger (Hope College, Mich.) and Harold Heie. Vern Visick (New College—Madison, Wis.) presented a response to Dr. Emmerich's paper. John Wilson, editor of *Books & Culture,* served as the reporter for this event as well as for the two subsequent case study events, with his reports appearing in the *Books & Culture* segment of the *Christianity Today* web site.

In October 2005, Paul DeWeese was the featured case-study speaker at Calvin College (Mich.), with the event co-sponsored by the Paul. B. Henry Institute for the Study of Christianity & Politics at Calvin College (Corwin Smidt, Director). Titled "Confrontational Politics versus Finding Principled Common Ground," this event was convened by Stephen Monsma and

Corwin Smidt. The responses to Dr. DeWeese's paper were presented by Amy Black (Wheaton College, Ill.) and a panel consisting of Vern Ehlers (U.S. House of Representatives), Bill Hardiman (Michigan House of Representatives), George Heartwell (Mayor, Grand Rapids, Mich.), and Jerry Kooiman (Michigan House of Representatives).

In May 2005, Jim Waller was the featured case study speaker at Whitworth College (Wash.), with the event co-sponsored by the Weyerhaeuser Center for Christian Faith & Learning at Whitworth College (Dale Soden, Director). This event was convened by George Marsden (University of Notre Dame, Ind.) and Dale Soden. The respondents were Julia Stronks (Whitworth College) and Ron White (former Dean of San Francisco Theological Seminary).

We express our deep appreciation to all those persons and institutions named above for their strong contribution to this CCS project. We also wish to thank Dan Russ, the present Director of the Center for Christian Studies, for his strong support of the initial project, as well as Debbie Drost and Jeremy Martin, staff members at the Center for Christian Studies, for their excellent handling of many of the logistical details of these case-study events.

Mutual
TREASURE

Chapter 1

CALLED TO BE SALT AND LIGHT: AN OVERVIEW

Stephen V. Monsma

Stephen V. Monsma is a research fellow at the Henry Institute for the Study of Christianity and Politics, Calvin College (Grand Rapids, Mich.) and a professor emeritus of political science at Pepperdine University (Malibu, Calif.) where he was on the political science faculty from 1987 to 2004 and held the Blanche E. Seaver chair in social science. He is also a non-resident scholar at the Institute for Studies of Religion at Baylor University.

Monsma has published widely in the fields of public policy, church-state relations, and faith-based nonprofit organizations. His most recent book is *Healing for a Broken World: Christian Perspectives on Public Policy* (2008). Among his other works are *Faith, Hope and Jobs: Welfare-to-Work in Los Angeles* (with J. Christopher Soper, 2006); *Putting Faith in Partnerships: Welfare-to-Work in Four Cities* (2004); *The Challenge of Pluralism: Church and State in Five Democracies* (with J. Christopher Soper, 1997; 2nd. ed. 2008); *When Sacred and Secular Mix: Religious Nonprofit Organizations and Public Money* (1996); and *Positive Neutrality* (1993). He has also published articles in such journals as the *Journal of Church and State, Policy Studies Review,* and *Notre Dame Journal of Law, Ethics, and Public Policy.*

You are the salt of the earth. But if the salt loses its saltiness, how can it be made salty again? It is no longer good for anything, except to be thrown out and trampled underfoot. You are the light of the world. A city on a hill cannot be hidden. Neither do people light a lamp and put it under a bowl. Instead they put it on its stand, and it gives light to everyone in the house. In the same way, let your light shine before others, that they may see your good deeds and glorify your Father in heaven.
—Matthew 5:13-14[1]

Christians who take the teachings of the Bible as God's truth agree that the call of Jesus Christ to be salt and light in the world is not optional.[2] In every time and place, Christians are expected to respond obediently to this call. This much is clear. Less clear is precisely how Christians should respond.

This book addresses the *how* question. How should Christians who take the Bible authoritatively and accept the basics of the historic Christian faith seek to influence the culture in which God has placed us? We need to "be as shrewd as snakes and as innocent as doves" (Matt. 10:16). But what does that mean in twenty-first-century North America? Ought we to thunder out the judgments of God as an Old Testament prophet? Or ought we to develop a stealth strategy that accepts as much of a secular worldview as possible and then slip in some Christian corrections here and there? Or maybe we should put first things first and concentrate on saving souls. After all, the worlds of scholarship, public policies, and feature films will soon come to an end, while the souls that have been saved for Christ will live forever.

Such are the questions this book addresses. It does not do so merely by way of abstract theories but by way of living, concrete case studies. In this first essay I set the context for these case studies by making four very basic points. First, I contend that working to influence the wider culture of society is an essential aspect of Christians presenting the full gospel of Christ's redeeming love. Second, I propose that in doing so we ought normally not to follow a confrontational approach that is abrasive and unyielding. Third, I make a case for an approach to cultural influence based on a dialogue model. Fourth, I note the exceptional circumstances when a confrontational approach may be appropriate.

CHRISTIANS AS GOD'S AGENTS FOR HIS REDEMPTIVE PURPOSES

As we observe the world in which we have been placed, two things are clear. One is that this earth is a place of undeniable beauty and joy. Think of the beauties of nature: surf breaking on a tropical beach, snow-capped mountain peaks, the call of birds breaking the stillness of the Florida Everglades. Or think of parents marveling at the tiny, perfectly formed fingers and toes of a newborn baby; or of a carpenter finding joy in turning raw wood into an object of beauty and usefulness; or of an elderly couple growing old together and rejoicing in grandchildren and even great-grandchildren God has given them.

But we also know this earth, as Cornelius Plantinga has put it, is not the way it is supposed to be.[3] Human sin has deeply marred it. Some parents cause their children's death through abuse and neglect; others subject their children to emotional and sexual abuse. Some carpenters defraud their customers and cut corners to make a few extra dollars. Some couples never grow old together because cancer or other disease cuts short one of their lives, leaving the other to grow old alone. Or selfishness, unfaithfulness, or simple disinterest kills the marriage years before the divorce court ratifies what has already taken place. The natural creation has also been affected by sin. Some species of plants and animals God has created are driven to extinction by human exploitation. Adam was told, "Cursed is the ground because of you; through painful toil you will eat of it all the days of your life" (Gen. 3:17). The apostle Paul in Romans declares, "We know that the whole creation has been groaning in the pains of childbirth right up to the present time" (Rom. 8:22). Paul also refers to the creation waiting "in eager expectation for the children of God to be revealed," and to "be liberated from its bondage to decay" (Rom. 8:19, 21).

The Christian message, however, does not stop with sin and its effects. It goes on to the story of redemption: how God through Christ is once again setting things right. Christ—through his birth, life, death, and resurrection—is reconciling the world unto God. The important message to understand is that this redeeming work of Christ was not limited to saving individuals from eternal punishment and assuring them of eternal life. Just as sin has affected all human relationships and even the natural creation, so also Christ's redeeming work transforms all human relationships and the natural creation.

This comprehensive view of God's redemptive purposes certainly includes the intention that all persons be reconciled to him. But God's redemptive purposes are much broader than that. God intends that persons and groups in conflict experience reconciliation and peace; that the poor, marginalized, and oppressed of the world receive justice; that human life thrive and blossom; that the world's physical and ecological environment flourish; that human beings gain greater understanding of all aspects of the created order so that they may live in proper relationship with that order; that human beings show appreciation for beauty in God's creation and foster the further creation of such beauty through their artistic endeavors. We can turn to Cornelius Plantinga again: "The whole world belongs to God, the whole world has fallen, and so the whole world needs to be redeemed—every last person, place, organization, and program."[4]

One additional crucial point: God has entrusted to Christians everywhere—to his church—this message of reconciliation. The apostle Paul refers to God "reconciling the world to himself in Christ." He then goes on to write: "All this is from God, who reconciled us to himself through Christ *and gave us the ministry of reconciliation.* . . . We are therefore Christ's ambassadors, as though God were making his appeal through us." (2 Cor. 5:18-20, emph. added.)

The conclusion is inescapable: We are called to mold and shape our culture, to be God's means of reconciliation in a world too much marred by alienation, disorder, and exploitation. It staggers the imagination to think that one day when Christ returns in power, God's redemptive purposes will be fully realized. It is our Christian hope that the day will soon come when human conflict, injustice, oppression, killing, a polluted environment, ignorance, and ugliness will be no more. What is the Christian calling in the meantime? We are called to create intimations, or precursors, of that full glory to come by being agents for God's redemptive purposes, each in accordance with his or her particular gifts and social location.

In seeking to be agents for God's redemptive purposes—to be salt and light in this world—it is important that many Christians earnestly engage the larger culture through active involvement in all forms of public discourse. Our witness to the good news of the gospel is truncated if all Christians only seek to save individual souls and not to witness to the healing power of the gospel to transform all facets of society with their fractured relationships. This is what being a molder or shaper of culture is all about.

THE CONFRONTATIONAL APPROACH TO INFLUENCING CULTURE

One approach to engaging culture is through confronting the errors of that culture forcefully and boldly. Sometimes this is called speaking prophetically, following the model of Old Testament prophets such as Isaiah and Amos who did not mince their words in condemning the sins of the ancient Israelites and their rulers.

The confrontational approach is marked by three characteristics. First is stridency. Persons use strong, harsh words as they put forward their positions and condemn those who disagree with them.

Second, no room is left for compromise and dialogue. Prophets have the answer; their attitude is, "I know I am right and you are wrong, so take it or leave it, but don't expect me to meet you halfway or seek to understand why you believe as you do."

Third, the confrontational approach tends to use the Bible in a proof-texting manner to support one's own position and to condemn the other's position. One puts forward one or more Bible verses that support one's position, and that settles that. Other biblical passages or the overall message of the Bible that may cast a different perspective on one's position are ignored. Also, instead of seeking to build bridges toward their opponents, such prophets blame those who do not accept the authority of the Bible. "If you reject what God tells us in the Bible, that's your problem, not mine," is the unspoken attitude.

There may be rare occasions when a confrontational approach may be appropriate, and I will consider them later. But such occasions are the exception, not the norm. The usual danger is that we will be confrontational when other means are called for, not that we will fail to be confrontational when we should be.

It is understandable why many are tempted by the confrontational mode of engagement with those with whom we disagree. Convinced that we have the truth on the issue at hand, what option do we have other than to present our belief in an unyielding manner? Anything else will be too timid and will fail to win others' attention. This mode of engagement may be especially tempting for Christians, who believe our position is God's and supported by the Bible. There are, however, at least three problems with this confrontational mode of engagement with those with whom we disagree.

First, it is an expression of hubris that denies human finitude. No human being has a God's-eye view. We all see "only a reflection as in a mirror" (1 Cor. 13:12). Our perspectives are partial, often reflecting aspects of our social location such as our gender, ethnicity, socio-economic status, the multiple traditions in which we are embedded, and our personal biographies. Therefore, we can and should learn from other human beings who have differing perspectives on the issue at hand.

Here it is important to distinguish between the eternal truths of Scripture and their applications in specific cultural settings. God's truths are sure and eternal; our applications of those truths in our cultural setting are limited and fallible. The sinfulness of human nature is a fact clear to any Christian who takes the teachings of Scripture as true. Anyone who doubts this need do no more than to look into his or her own heart.

But how ought we apply this truth in a specific setting? For example, how should it guide our evaluations of a feature film filled with graphic violence? Condemn it as glorifying violence and seeking to make money by shocking viewers drawn to films that "push the envelope"? Or praise it as graphically demonstrating the depths of evil to which humankind can sink without the redeeming grace of God? Even answers to questions as straightforward as these will reveal differences of opinion among equally sincere Christians—and between Christians and thoughtful nonbelievers. Questions of public policies, academic interpretations, and literary criticism usually come in forms more complex than this one example. In such situations hubris is a fault all ought to seek to avoid.

Second, confrontation usually is not an effective way to change persons and their opinions. It is counter-productive. The confrontational clash of positions seldom changes anyone's mind. More typically it entrenches adherents in their original positions, often creating animosity and escalating ill will in its wake. When our opinions and the way we are used to thinking are suddenly condemned as being totally wrong, the very human reaction is to dig in our heels and work hard to prove the other person wrong. Our opinions become more fixed. We feel that not just our positions are being attacked, but also that we ourselves are being attacked. The closing of one's mind and resistance are the natural reactions. In addition, quoting Bible texts to someone who does not accept the authority of the Bible will obviously not get one very far.

Then when our confrontational efforts do not result in other persons changing their positions, Christians are tempted to withdraw from efforts to influence others in the broader culture, blame them for rejecting the clear truth, and feel self-righteous about recognizing the truth those others are so stubbornly rejecting. We fail to recognize the other persons' rejection may have less to do with their stubborness and more to do with the way we presented our position.

Third, for those who claim to be followers of Jesus, confrontation is simply not a Christian way to engage other people. Jesus calls Christians to love others (Matt. 22: 34-40). An oft-neglected aspect of loving another person who disagrees with you is to create a welcoming space for that person to express disagreement, to work empathetically to understand the other's position by putting yourself in is or her shoes, then to talk respectfully about your disagreements, starting with any common ground you may share, in the hope of learning from one another.

To commit ourselves to loving the person with whom we disagree is not to compromise our strong convictions about our own beliefs. It is to embrace both poles of a rare combination pointed to by Ian Barbour in his definition of religious maturity: "It is by no means easy to hold beliefs for which you would be willing to die, and yet to remain open to new insights; but it is precisely such a combination of commitment and inquiry that constitutes religious maturity."[5] Openness to the beliefs of others without commitment to your own beliefs too easily leads to sheer relativism. Commitment without openness too easily leads to fanaticism, even terrorism. As C. S. Lewis has observed, and recent world events illustrate, "Those who are readiest to die for a cause may easily become those who are readiest to kill for it."[6] One of the most pressing needs in our world today is for all human beings to embrace, and hold in tension, both commitment and openness.

For Christians, our call is for "speaking the truth [as we understand it] in love" (Eph. 4:15). In that process we then are to exemplify the Christian virtues of humility and patience, daring to believe that in the very process of such respectful conversation the gift of a greater understanding of the truth may emerge.

THE DIALOGUE MODEL OF CULTURAL ENGAGEMENT

In contrast both to failing to attempt to influence culture and to confronting culture in confrontational, uncompromising terms is the dialogue model of cultural engagement. This model is based on an honest, genuine, thoughtful dialogue with those with whom one disagrees. It consists of a three-step process. The first step is *establishing a spirit of mutual trust and respect with those with whom one disagrees*. This can be achieved in two ways. One consists of establishing personal, face-to-face relationships with persons holding views opposite one's own. This will often involve reaching across the racial, partisan, academic, social class, sexual orientation, religious, and other such lines that separate us. It aims to get to know on a personal level those with whom we disagree and whose positions we are planning to critique. This is not easy for many of us to do. But it is crucial.

If, for example, one is planning to criticize the legalization of same-sex marriages for which gay activists are working, the dialogue model says one first needs to establish a personal relationship with one or more of the gay activists who are supporting same-sex marriage. Then one will see them as persons; one will be in a position to understand what values, assumptions, hopes, resentments, and beliefs are underlying the position you believe is wrong. Or if an academic is convinced a certain trend in the academy is flatly contrary to a biblical worldview, she should first get to know someone taking that position, take him out for lunch, find out what makes that person tick, get to know him as a person—and let him get to know her as a person. Or the dialogue approach says persons in political positions should first establish personal friendships with persons of the opposite party or a different faction of their own party. The examples could be multiplied indefinitely.

There is a second way to establish an atmosphere of mutual respect and trust with those with whom you disagrees. It is—even in the absence of personal, face-to-face relationships—to engage in dialogue in a thoughtful, honest, respectful manner in your writings, speeches, or artistic endeavors. It means presenting the views of those with whom you disagree in a factually accurate manner, not attacking their motives, leaving open the possibility of your changing your position if convinced you are wrong, and communicating in a balanced, thoughtful manner. Doing so will likely lead to a spirit of mutual respect and trust—a foundation on which further fruitful dialogue can be built, just as face-to-face, interpersonal relationships can.

Establishing mutual trust and respect with someone with whom you disagree—and he or she with you—has two positive results. First, this makes it harder to write off the other person, and the other person will have a harder time writing you off, as stupid, biased, or evil. It becomes harder for persons in a dispute to demonize the other as foolish or bad. This, in turn, is likely to decrease name-calling and generate more honest representations by both sides of the other side's positions. Typically, in cultural disputes the tendency is to put the other side in as negative a light as possible, and then mount an attack based on the negative portrait. This makes the attack easier and more likely to stir up righteous indignation. But it will also deepen the alienation of the other person. When you personally know persons on the other side, and they know you, or when you publically address them in honest, thoughtful terms, you and they are much more likely to speak in more measured, fairer terms.

But this step of establishing a spirit of mutual trust and respect with those with whom one disagrees means one must be prepared both to earn and to give respect. One can disagree strongly and insistently with someone else, and yet respect that person. For Christians that respect comes, first, from a realization that the other person is an image bearer of almighty God; he or she is a child of God.

In addition, it comes from a sense of humility and a realization that our own sinful nature means we see only partly—and with lenses clouded by our self-interests and fears. Our knowledge and understanding of the truth are never so complete and clear as to block our being able to learn from someone else. Understanding the other and what has shaped him or her can be the beginning of greater insight.

A second step in the dialogue model is an extension of the first step: *coming to understand why those who are opposed to us take the positions that we see as being wrong.* This means either truly coming to know on a personal level individuals with whom we disagree or listening to their public positions with genuinely open hearts and minds. What are they thinking? What are their reasons for taking the positions they do? What are they seeing that you may have missed? And what have you seen that they are missing? How can you encourage them to see important facts and perspectives crucial to a biblical view but to which they are oblivious?

We should always be asking ourselves why the other person has taken what we are convinced is a wrong course. Why is it that gay activists wish for the government to give its blessing to gay unions by labeling them marriages? Why is a Richard Dawkins convinced that God is indeed a delusion?[7] Why are some environmentalists convinced that earth is our Mother and human beings are on the same level with plants and animals? Why is a political conservative convinced taxes need to be cut, when you see millions of persons in desperate need of additional government services?

As we can answer questions such as these, we are in a better position to dialogue with persons taking a position opposite to our own. We will know what common ground we may share and how we can use it to win confidence or respect and then encourage our conversation partners to see the biblically based insights and perspectives to which we hold. Also, we may discover perspectives that we have missed. We may find we need to reconsider and perhaps modify some aspects of our own position.

This, in turn, may lead to the third step in the dialogue approach to influencing culture: that of *persons on the other side altering their position—or you, perhaps, altering your position—so as to reach greater, even if not complete, agreement.* The hope is that out of the mutual trust and respect and greater understanding of the other side's position growing out of an honest exchange of views, larger areas of agreement and a modification of positions may result. Usually when this occurs, it will start by identification of some common ground or areas of agreement. Maybe you will discover that your goals are similar but you differ on the means to reach those goals. Or maybe you can find different means that neither of you had seen and ones on which you can agree. Discovering greater areas of agreement will not always happen, but it is much more likely to happen through the dialogue than the confrontational approach. Persons will not be thrown onto the defensive or have to admit they were totally wrong.

Under the dialogue model, one starts with trust and respect, moves to an understanding of what motivations and perspectives underlie the differing positions, and from there finds areas of common ground and larger areas of agreement. Christians—if we know what we believe and why—can engage in this model without putting our commitment to the central teachings of Scripture up for grabs. The dialogue model is indeed a matter of dialogue, not a relativistic model that puts all truth claims on the same level.

I do not want to sound Pollyannaish, as though the world is completely populated by reasonable persons who will always respond to offers to establish personal relationships and dialogue. I have spent almost all my adult life in academia and in active politics. In both arenas, I have experienced persons who are arrogant, self-centered, opinionated, and anything but open to dialogue of any kind. This has not been true of most persons, but it has been true of some. For such persons the dialogue model is unlikely to work well.

But even in relation to such persons I suggest three reasons to follow the dialogue model in most situations. First, even when our positions are rejected, dialogue may earn new understanding of and respect for our positions. I once attended a conference at which one of the speakers—clearly a bright, thoughtful person—railed against the biblical teaching of the awful reality of hell. She could not see how any rational person could believe in the existence of hell. But it also became clear to me that she was not reacting against an understanding of the Christian teaching of hell with any depth of insight or understanding. She had a third-grader's understanding of hell. She was therefore repulsed by this doctrine and easily and airily dismissed it. The dialogue model would help to prevent this. If she had been in touch with Christian believers who had respectfully discussed with her thoughtful Christian understandings of hell and how they can fit with an all-good, loving God, she still might not have accepted the existence of a hell, but she would no longer have been able to dismiss it out of hand along with the tooth fairy, Santa Claus, and other fantasies of nine-year-olds. As those who take opposite positions to ours on religious and cultural issues of the day gain a deeper understanding and more respect for our Christian positions, the way may be opened for them eventually to accept other teachings of Christianity and, in God's own time, our Savior.

A second reason to pursue the dialogue model even when it is unlikely to greatly alter others' positions is that it honors our Lord and Savior. It is the way of peace, of turning the other cheek, of building bridges, of reconciliation. "What would Jesus do?" can be overused as a guide to moral action. But it has its strengths. It is hard for me to picture Jesus standing outside an abortion clinic railing against women coming there for abortions, picketing the homes of doctors who perform abortions with "Baby killer" signs, or distorting the positions of his opponents to score debating points. I think he would be much more likely to come alongside the women obtaining abortions to find out what was moving them to make such a choice. Or he might sit down with an abortion provider and seek to understand what had moved him to make a living in this manner, then gently but insistently suggest a better way. Or he would be more concerned for the eternal welfare of someone disagreeing with him than with publically humiliating him or her. Even when our voices are rejected and spurned, we are following our Lord's way and honoring him.

This leads to a third reason to pursue the dialogue approach to cultural engagement, even on occasions when it may seem ineffective. It is that God will make use of our faithful efforts in his own time to accomplish his own purposes. We must remind ourselves that God is in charge, not us. It is not our job to wring cultural change out of the present situation by our own efforts. To think this is to think in triumphalistic terms. We are to offer our lives in faithful service to our Lord. He will make use of our proffered service to accomplish his purposes. As we pursue the dialogue model, maybe the only change—and the one God most desires—is in ourselves as we faithfully and humbly seek to shape our culture in God-approved ways. Our culture may not change at all, but we will. And that is good. Even when it appears our efforts are having no effect, we may have planted seeds in the minds and hearts of others that will bear fruit decades later. We may not see any results of our efforts in our lifetimes, but later—at a time of God's choosing—there may be spectacular results. Or maybe not.

We are called to faithful service as culture bearers and shapers. This, I am convinced, in most circumstances means pursuing the dialogue model of cultural engagement. But after faithfully following this model to the best of our ability, we need to let go and let God use our faithful service to accomplish his will.

WHEN CONFRONTATION IS CALLED FOR

Earlier I mentioned "What would Jesus do?" as a standard sometimes useful to gauge the morality and appropriateness of our actions. If this has any validity, I must recognize that Jesus sometimes used the confrontational approach. This is most vividly seen in Matthew 23:

> Woe to you, teachers of the law and Pharisees, you hypocrites! You give a tenth of your spices—mint, dill and cumin. But you have neglected the more important matters of the law—justice, mercy and faithfulness. You should have practiced the latter, without neglecting the former. You blind guides! You strain out a gnat but swallow a camel.
>
> Woe to you, teachers of the law and Pharisees, you hypocrites! You clean the outside of the cup and dish, but inside they are full of greed and self-indulgence. Blind Pharisee! First clean the inside of the cup and dish ,then the outside also will be clean. (Matt. 23:23-26)

This is hardly an example of the dialogue model I have been calling for!

But contrast this with Jesus' approach to the Samaritan woman at the well. (John 4:4-42.) She clearly was a sinner, living with a man who was not her husband. She asked naïve questions. But Jesus did not confront and condemn. He followed the dialogue model. He established a personal relationship with her, answered her questions, and gently led her toward facing the immoral life she was living.

Christ is a model of both the confrontational and the dialogue approach. How are we to know which one we ought to use when? I have two comments. First, Jesus almost always used the dialogue model, not the confrontational model. I cited the example of the Samaritan woman at the well, but I could easily cite many other examples. Think of Nicodemus who came to Jesus at night, of Zacchaeus to whose house Jesus came, of the despised tax collector Matthew whom Jesus called to follow him, of the rich young ruler whom Jesus also called to follow, and on and on. Such examples suggest to me that the dialogue approach ought to be the default position, and that we should invoke the confrontational approach only when certain special circumstances call for it.

My second comment is that—using Matthew 23 as a guide— there seem to be three special circumstances in that situation that led Jesus to use the confrontational model. One is that those whom he confronted knew better. Jesus did not confront the uneducated, ordinary persons but the religious leaders and experts in the Mosaic law. They knew the law; they knew the prophets. They should have known from Isaiah, Amos, and other resources that God asks first and foremost for clean hearts, for acts of justice and mercy, not a legalistic following of the outwards forms of the law.

Second, those whom Jesus confronted had persisted in their actions. The condemnations of Matthew 23 came near the end of Christ's ministry on earth. They had heard Jesus parables, they had seen him eat with notorious sinners, they had seen him perform miracles. Yet they just did not get it. They persisted in their ways, even though the truth was there and had been presented to them.

Third, the persons Jesus confronted were in positions of influence and leadership. They were leading others who were less educated and less sophisticated astray.

From this I would suggest that confrontational tactics are most frequently called for when the persons being confronted already have an accurate understanding of the Christian truth, have persistently rejected it, and are in positions of leadership where they are leading many others astray. Even then prudence should lead one to ask whether or not dialogue based on a person-to-person relationship might not be more effective. But prudence may indicate that confrontation is justified.

THE REST OF THE BOOK

This chapter has, of necessity, been long on theory and positions that may appear abstract to some. I myself like to think in terms of concrete examples. To me—and I suspect to many others—more theoretical points take on flesh and blood and come to life when actual, living examples are given. That is what the rest of this book does. By way of living case studies both the value and the limits of the dialogue model will be fleshed out and brought to life.

However I recognize the limitations of case studies. They cannot always be generalized. A case study may prove a point only for the case being presented. So, I will not claim that these case studies prove the efficacy of the proposed three-step model for dialogue. Rather, I make the more modest suggestion that they may give you a partial glimpse of the dynamics of these three steps in a few concrete cases, for all of which there seem to have been some redemptive results.

As you read these case studies, ask yourself what in them illustrate the three steps in the dialogue model: establishing an atmosphere of mutual trust and respect, exchanging views, and modifying previously held positions. Then ask what all this means for you as God is calling you to be an agent for reconciliation in the setting in which he has placed you.

NOTES

1. All the biblical quotations in this essay are from the NIV, *Today's New International Version*.

2. This essay makes use of some portions of an earlier unpublished essay written by Harold Heie, the co-editor of this volume. I am in-

debted to him for allowing me to use portions of his essay. I am, however, solely responsible for any errors or improper interpretations contained in this essay.

3. Cornelius Plantinga Jr., *Not the Way It is Supposed to Be: A Brevity on Sin* (Grand Rapids, Mich.: Eerdmans, 1995).

4. Cornelius Plantinga Jr., *Engaging God's World* (Grand Rapids, Mich.: Eerdmans, 2002), p. 98.

5. Ian Barbour, *Myths, Models, and Paradigms: A Comparative Study in Science and Religion* (New York: Harper & Row, 1974), p. 138.

6. C. S. Lewis, *Reflections on the Psalms* (New York: Harcourt, Brace & World, 1958), p. 28.

7. The reference is to Richard Dawkins' bestselling book, *The God Delusion* (Boston: Houghton Mifflin Harcourt, 2006).

Chapter 2

"GETTING INTO THE LOAF": ENGAGING THE SECULAR ACADEMY

James E. Waller

Dr. James Waller is an Affiliated Scholar with the Auschwitz Institute for Peace and Reconciliation. He received his B.S. (1983) from Asbury College (Ky.), M.S. (1985) from the University of Colorado, and Ph.D. (1988) from the University of Kentucky.

Waller is a widely recognized scholar in the field of Holocaust and genocide studies. He has held international visiting professorships at the Technical University in Berlin (1990) and the Catholic University in Eichstatt, Germany (1992) as well as participated in international Holocaust seminars hosted by the Stanley Burton Center for Holocaust Studies at the University of Leicester in England (2006) and the Institute of Sociology at Jagiellonian University in Krakow, Poland (2007). Waller has been awarded summer fellowships and been a teaching fellow with the Holocaust Educational Foundation at Northwestern University (1996, 2007) and at the Center for Advanced Holocaust Studies at the U.S. Holocaust Memorial Museum in Washington, D.C. (1999, 2003, and 2005).

Waller's book on perpetrators of genocide, *Becoming Evil: How Ordinary People Commit Genocide and Mass Killing* (Oxford

University Press, 2002), was praised by *Publisher's Weekly* for "clearly and effectively synthesizing a wide range of studies to develop an original and persuasive model of the process by which people can become evil." In addition to being used as a textbook in college and university courses around the world, *Becoming Evil* also was short-listed for the biennial Raphael Lemkin Award from the International Association of Genocide Scholars and was released in a revised and updated second edition in March 2007. A Hungarian translation of *Becoming Evil* is scheduled for release in April 2009.

INTRODUCTION

When I began my teaching career in a Christian college in 1985, I quickly knew that this was the context in which I wished to immerse my professional self as a *teacher*. I thrived on the freedom to explore issues of faith and learning in an environment that prized each. It was clear that, as a teacher, there was no other context as conducive for me in engaging students—regardless of their faith orientation—as was that of a Christian college. Less clear for me, however, was the issue of what type of audience I should be engaging as a *scholar*. In taking seriously my vocation as a Christian teacher-scholar, I had to ask myself, Who am I called to engage as a scholar? And how am I called to engage them? Should I speak as a Christian scholar to other Christians, with a particular focus on the Christian academy? Or should I speak as a Christian scholar to other scholars (regardless of faith orientation) with a particular focus on the secular academy?

It is clear that this bifurcation between Christian and secular is too simple and too artificial. It is as ridiculous to believe that one can think only with a Christian lens, unfiltered by any secular influence, as it is to believe that one can think only with a secular lens, unfiltered by any faith influence. It is just as clear, however, that in practice most scholars, at various points in their professional careers, face the dilemma of professional location, involvement, and emphasis exactly in this manner: Who are we called to engage, and how are we called to engage them?

For this chapter to have any meaning, some understanding of my record of engagement in both academies is necessary. I will be the first to admit that I do not have a notable track record of successful engagement with the Christian academy. For instance, like many young Christian teacher-scholars, I just defaulted to the notion that my first book should be published with a Christian press. It was with great confidence that I submitted the manuscript, focusing on issues of race in America, to every known Christian publishing house. It was with equally great embarrassment that I experienced being turned away by every one—with the notable quote from one rejection letter that race in America was "no longer a problem in which Christians need be interested."

With the possible exception of this essay, I can think of few other published pieces I've placed in Christian publications. This doesn't stop Christians (unfortunately, at times) from responding to my work. Of all the reviews of my most recent book, *Becoming Evil: How Ordinary People Commit Genocide and Mass Killing* [1], the two most negative have come from Christians—one from a liberal Christian perspective unable to stomach the notion of something inherent in human nature that makes us all capable of committing evil, the other from a conservative Christian perspective that agreed with the fallenness of human nature but took issue with my methodology (evolutionary psychology).

Similarly, I'll often find that the toughest audiences for me to engage as a speaker—whether in relation to my work on race relations or genocide studies—are Christian audiences. Whether it be speaking to a group of chief academic officers from the Council for Christian Colleges and Universities (CCCU), delivering a Staley Lecture Series at a CCCU-affiliated institution, being a workshop leader for CCCU faculty seminars on faith-learning integration, or simply speaking at church retreats or delivering a guest sermon, there are just too many points at which it seems as if I and the Christian audience are speaking a different language.

It's not that I don't enjoy these engagements; as a matter of fact, the challenges they raise make me enjoy them greatly. It's just that it's not my easiest, and certainly not my most natural, connection. It feels as if it simply takes a lot more work for me to find with most Christian audiences that common point of connection essential to effective engagement.

By nature I am much more comfortable pointing out my own shortcomings. However, I do need to make the contrasting case for my relative success in engaging the secular academy. If I don't do so, at least briefly, there will be little reason for anyone to be interested in whatever I may say about engaging the secular academy. So, in addition to over fifty peer-reviewed articles and chapters in secular journals and edited volumes, I've now had published four books, all with secular presses, all well-received.[2] (The first book, eventually published as *Face to Face: The Changing State of Racism in America*,[3] even attracted some Christian readers who evidently believe race is a problem in which the church should still be interested.) Two of those four books have been short-listed for national or international book awards. *Becoming Evil*, first published by Oxford University Press in 2002, has now been published in a second edition and is used as a textbook in more than fifty college and university courses around the world. *Becoming Evil* is even being adapted for a play in the UCLA theater department and is prominently featured as a significant plot device (not simply a blunt piece of weaponry) in a best-selling Danish novel.

Each year I enjoy the opportunity of numerous speaking engagements and invited addresses at secular campuses and universities. I'm a regular part of teaching teams at high-level faculty seminars on the Holocaust and genocide studies at the U.S. Holocaust Museum in D.C. and at Northwestern University in Illinois. I have no shortage of opportunities to be on panels related to issues of diversity at a wide range of secular institutions—both inside and outside of higher education. In short, the same material—whether on race relations or genocide studies—that often falls flat for Christian audiences seems in high demand for secular audiences; it feels as if we are speaking the same language. I find easily that common point of connection that makes for effective engagement.

Of course, neither the criticism in Christian circles nor the acclaim in secular circles is universal; these are simply broadbrush characterizations of my self-perceived reception in two separate if overlapping academies. In general, though, and for whatever reasons, I have little or nothing to say about engaging the Christian academy because I clearly do such a poor job of it. Fortunately, there are scores of other thoughtful and intelligent Christian thinkers who engage the Christian academy in important and meaningful ways; the fact that I have yet to figure out those ways for myself points not to their lack of importance but to my own shortcomings.

More than anything, these experiences—both humbling and encouraging—are mirrors that reflect back to me my own comfort zones and points of influence. Based on this, my chapters explores three questions related to engaging the secular academy. First, what motivates me to engage the secular academy; why is it so important in my understanding of my vocation as a Christian teacher-scholar? Second, what is my model of engagement with the secular academy? Third, what are the risks of this model of engagement?

WHAT MOTIVATES ME TO ENGAGE THE SECULAR ACADEMY?

Early in my career, two distant mentors—David Myers and Mary Stewart Van Leeuwen—became pivotal in my understanding of my vocation as a Christian teacher-scholar. While, at this point in my career, I've come to know both of these colleagues fairly well and have written with one (Myers) and taught with the other (Van Leeuwen[4]), it was a point-counterpoint set of articles (including, as well, responses from John Yeatts and James Foster) between the two that helped crystalize my vision of who I was called to engage and how I was called to engage them. Resonating most deeply with me was Myer's concluding assertion that

> we need more Christian scholars not in the stands but down on the playing field . . . let there also be Christians who, by getting into the game, provide their witness to the larger intellectual community. If we are to be the "leaven in the loaf" we must get into the loaf. As C. S. Lewis once declared, "We do not need more Christian books; we need more books by Christians about everything with Christian values built in."[5]

Myers closed that piece with an earlier quote from Nicholas Wolterstorff that equally gave voice to my calling. Wolterstorff urged the Christian psychologist to occupy the academy

> not . . . as one who surveys the scene from outside and now and then makes some clucking noises, but as one who participates in the nitty-gritty of actual psychological explorations. Do not just be a critic. Be a creative initiator, faithful in your thinking.[6]

In part because of these influences, I've long taken the "nitty-gritty"[7] of "getting into the loaf" seriously. Even when I was an associate editor for *Christian Scholars Review*, for example, I retained the right to encourage authors of particularly good submissions to seek publication in secular journals rather than in the pages of *CSR*. In other words, I would occasionally get articles that were simply too good to confine to the Christian academy and deserved, even demanded, a wider dissemination in the secular academy. (One can imagine some of the responses I got to those types of "rejection" letters.)

For me, this motivation to engage the secular academy fits within a broader understanding of how Christians might engage culture. More than fifty years ago, H. Richard Niebuhr, in what has become a "contested classic," outlined five typical answers to the Christian's problem of seeing the relation between the Christ she calls Lord and the culture which holds her as the sea holds its fish.[8] In his concept of "Christ the Transformer of Culture," Niebuhr maintained that Christians could seek to re-create the culture in which they live. Such a Christian is neither consumed with the world he is living in, nor by eternal life, but seeks to live between what God has already accomplished and what God has yet to finish. In this perspective, the Fall only perverted things which were created good, but these things remain inherently good and capable of reform—even though they have been misdirected. In sum, under Christ's transforming guidance, reason and faith are powerful means of finding truth. For me, this means that engaging the secular academy is legitimate, perhaps even mandatory, for those with the abilities to do so. Finally, for me, this means that engaging the secular academy is participating in God's work of restoring the original goodness of the Creation.[9]

Even more cogent than Niebuhr's typology, to my mind, is Judaism's two-word summary of human beings' obligations to each other—*Tikkun Olam*. Tikkun Olam is one of the 613 Mitzvot, or divine commands, in Jewish tradition, and refers to repairing the world (literally, "the reparation of the universe"). This medieval doctrine held that when the universe was created, moral flaws were inadvertently introduced into it. Thus evil and suffering became part of what was originally intended as a perfectly good universe. But these flaws are reversible. Jews are nothing less than partners with God, in that they have been charged with the task of uprooting evil and perfecting the cosmos that God created eons ago. We are thus called to reclaim our personal autonomy and help finish the good work that God began.

For many Jewish thinkers, including Gershom Scholem, *the* critical human task is that of repairing and mending the world.[10] This redemption of the world is not a spectacular intrusion from beyond but rather the "logical consequence" of the history of the world. Other Jewish thinkers even dare to suggest that, by engaging in Tikkun Olam, the mending of the broken world, we are actually helping to heal a wounded God as well. That is, God suffers in our suffering, and so it follows that anything we do to alleviate the sufferings we impose on each other also alleviates God's suffering.

This is why I see it as vital for Christians to take the nitty-gritty of getting into the loaf seriously by engaging the secular academy. As a counterexample, I think the failure of the Intelligent Design (ID) movement has involved not getting down on the playing field of the secular academy. Yes, some think ID a "success," but this is not due to its professional influence but only to its high-profile curricular challenges—which have been decisively discredited by the courts—in several school boards across the nation. Most (certainly not all) of the significant works on ID have been published by small Christian presses which are not exactly at home, nor do they have a respected voice in, the secular arena. In addition, the few professional conferences at which ID folk seem to have a presence are those that they sponsor themselves—which, on at least two occasions, have been misleadingly advertised to lure in secular folk (not the most intellectually or ethically respectable mode of engagement).

While ID proponents will claim that they haven't been "allowed" into the game, I maintain that their relegation is self-imposed and has been due to an ineffective model of engagement. While ID proponents still have a tenacious hold on public discourse, they have chosen to stand on the sidelines of academic debate with a shrill, dismissive, churlish, and arrogant tone. This has caused them to be left out of a discussion to which they could possibly make an important contribution—if only they would engage in ways that give them voice rather than take it away.

WHAT IS MY MODEL OF
ENGAGEMENT WITH THE SECULAR ACADEMY?

So, following on the heels of my criticism of ID's engagement with the secular academy, how do I propose to constructively engage the secular academy? The model I'll present has, I believe, worked well for me. It is, though, just *one* model out of many ways that Christians can engage the secular academy and will certainly not work equally well for everyone, perhaps not even me in a different season of my career.

My model is built around three forms of humility—worldview, intellectual, and relational. I should recognize here that every writer I've read on humility has seemed arrogant. The people who really should write about humility are those least likely to do so, and I certainly illustrate my own assertion more so than not. In my most honest of hours, I know that one of my greater weaknesses, among many, is lack of humility. Having acknowledged that, let me risk moving on. Each of these three forms of humility is best understood in the general context of an interpersonal, relational model in which engagement with ideas is, of necessity, engagement with the real people who hold those ideas.

Worldview Humility

To my mind, the most important sentence of Niebuhr's "contested classic" is the following: "All our faith is fragmentary, though we do not all have the same fragments of faith."[11] This summarizes well my own disinclinations toward "evangelical" as an apt descriptor of my faith perspective. It also summarizes well my own inclinations toward listening and bearing witness in a way that evidences a worldview humility able to recognize the fragmentary nature of my faith as well as the diversity of fragments of faith borne by those around me. For some, including my students and colleagues, these statements make me somehow less than what a Christian is supposed to be. I see this, however, as honest recognition of the fact that I hold my faith with *sufficient certainty*—but not with *absolute certainty*.

To borrow Alexis de Tocqueville's famous statement that true democracy is never absolutely sure it's right, true faith—for me—is also never absolutely sure it's right. That understanding has served me well as a reminder of worldview humility. As a result, I have the freedom to be as critical, if not more so, of religion than are my secular colleagues. I am as offended as they are by Christians who demand textual literalism when it suits them and supply their own interpretation otherwise. Few in the field of genocide studies have taken the church to task for its role in genocide as have I in my ongoing research. Similarly, the student study programs that I lead in Northern Ireland don't labor under the misguided notion that religion has not played any role in the sectarian violence of that region or that religion offers a ready healing antidote.

When I beat my secular colleagues to the punch in criticizing religion, it is not only disarming but also opens the window for me to express the hope of what religion can be in the human experience. In other words, my willingness to engage in self-critique (following Mark Noll's classic model in *The Scandal of the Evangelical Mind*, 1994) grants me the voice to then be apologetic and defensive as well as making the case for religion in the human experience. By being, as a Christian, self-critical of what Christianity *is*, I legitimize a voice for then holding out the promise of what Christianity *can be*.

I am motivated here by the distinction, captured by Cornel West, between what he terms *Constantinian Christianity* and *prophetic Christianity*.[12] For West, Constantinian Christianity is a "terrible merger of church and state" in which Christianity, driven by the arrogance of power and the tyranny of *is*, too often finds itself "on the wrong side of so many of our social troubles, such as the dogmatic justification of slavery and the parochial defense of women's inequality." Conversely, prophetic Christianity, driven by the humility of service and the vision of *can be*, battles imperialism and social injustice and aspires to represent the democratic ideal of religion in public life, as exemplified by such social activists as Dorothy Day (Catholic Worker Movement) and Ida B. Wells-Barnett (anti-lynching activist). For me, prophetic Christianity has embedded within it a worldview humility that is self-critical, self-reflective, and self-correcting as it aspires to the promise of what Christianity *can be*.

Intellectual Humility

Christianity is not for me some grand unifying theory, and I don't present it as such. As a Christian, I may certainly have "specialized cognitive access," as Wolterstorff and others have suggested, but that doesn't mean that my Christian worldview will inform *everything* I study—it's important to know when to say when.

For example, my doctoral dissertation focused on social loafing, that is, the reality that people reduce effort when working in a group compared to when working alone. In other words, why does a committee of twelve always seem to produce work comparable, in quantity and quality, to a non-group collection of six individuals? Certainly social loafing is an important topic in group dynamics, and finding solutions to reduce or eliminate it would mean corresponding increases in group efficiency. Just as certainly, however, there is little or nothing that my specialized cognitive access as a Christian scholar can bring to bear on this problem. In other words, what I see in social loafing as a scholar trained in group dynamics is no different than what I see in social loafing as a scholar who also happens to be Christian. I could search for portions of Scripture verses to tag to social loafing to somehow make it "Christian" scholarship—but that would be no less ridiculous than believing that, by singing a hymn at the beginning or end of class, one has somehow found the magic fount of what real faith-learning integration looks like.

Thus in some areas of research, like social loafing, I adopt what Ronald Nelson describes as a *compatibilist* strategy. Such an approach recognizes no deep, fundamental tension between the assumptions and procedures of my discipline and my Christian faith.[13]

There are other areas of my scholarship, however, in which the relationship between my discipline and my Christian faith is more problematic. In William Hasker's summary of Nelson's strategies, here I follow a *transformationist* strategy in which I find "the discipline to be lacking in insights and perspectives which are vital to [me] as a Christian."[14] I see this exemplified in my work on perpetrators of genocide and mass killing. In this work, focused not on architects of genocide or on mid-level bureaucrats but on the actual rank-and-file killers themselves, I am not the first person to ask how people come to enact such extraordinary evil. Some have responded to that question by emphasizing the extraordinary origins of such actions—the nature of the collective, ideology, psychopathology, or a twisted personality. Others, like me, have responded by highlighting the ordinary origins of extraordinary evil and trying to unpack the myriad factors that transform ordinary people, like you and me, into genocidal killers.

What has been conspicuously absent from the scholarly discussion, however, has been a serious consideration of the role of human nature in understanding perpetrator behavior. As Franklin Littell, emeritus professor of religion at Temple University, writes, "The hidden agenda is disagreement about the nature and destiny of Man, and of such mysteries as Sin and Evil."[15] By "human nature," I am referring to the fact that in some unique ways each of us is like *no other* human being. In other ways, each of us is like *some other* human beings. And in yet other ways, each of us is like *all other* human beings.

The question of the nature of human nature is captured in that final statement. In what ways are we like *every other* person who has gone before us and will come after us? Could there be a universal human condition that precedes all extraordinary evil and from which all extraordinary evil is derived? Christian readers will recognize this Augustinian notion of the historical corruption of our original goodness. In this view we are born with a flawed nature that, to fulfill itself, will inevitably commit evil. I believe the nature of human nature is pivotal to an understanding of how ordinary people commit genocide and mass killing and the modest success of my contribution to this discussion in the secular academy has been my attempt to bring this hidden agenda back into the scholarly discussion.

I want to be clear that, at least on the surface, my work in *Becoming Evil* certainly appears to be more compatibilist than transformationist. That is, while my assumptions about human nature are informed by my Christian faith, I also have to recognize that the vocabulary and methodology in which I am trained, and the vocabulary and methodology through which this discussion takes place in the secular academy, is not theological in nature. It would be intellectually irresponsible of me to attempt to make a theological argument related to human nature when I have a difficult time spelling "theological." Such an attempt, even were I to pull it off, would almost certainly fall on deaf ears in the secular academy. So, my *transformationist vision* is communicated through a *compatibilist strategy* of relying on the

vocabulary and methodology with which I am most familiar—
in this case, evolutionary psychology[16]—to make a case for the
role of human nature which the secular academy will be able to
hear and willing to engage (albeit not always warmly).

In sum, my mode of engagement with the secular academy
includes a mixture of compatibilist and transformationalist ele-
ments. When the area of study dictates that I work as a compatibilist, I proceed as everyone else does. I play the same game by
the same rules; the success of engagement depends on the
strength of my ideas, data, and argument. I pledge no specialized cognitive access under that strategy and have no need to
challenge the presuppositions of my discipline or the topic
under study.

When, however, the area of study invites a specialized cognitive access, I work as a transformationist, engaging the secular
academy as a scholar of faith. When proceeding as a transformationist, my hope is to bring insights and perspectives that transform my discipline or the topic under study. To do so requires
supplementing a worldview and intellectual humility with a relational humility that creates an interpersonal context in which
my voice, as a Christian scholar, can be heard as I seek to remedy
what I find to be lacking, or limited, in the vision of the secular
academy.

Relational Humility

As I mentioned earlier, engagement with ideas in the secular
academy is, of necessity, engagement with others (real people)
who carry those ideas. In that engagement, I try to practice (not
always successfully) a relational humility that leaves open
spaces for me and others to tear down the barriers of "us" and
"them" that too often hinder effective engagement.

Social psychologists often speak of "us" and "them" in the
context of "in-group" and "out-group." The in-group is any
group to which we belong or with which we identify. In-groups
can range from small, face-to-face groups of family and friends
to large social categories such as race, ethnicity, gender, or religion. Out-groups are any groups to which we do not belong or
with which we do not identify. Once these boundaries are established, we tend to be partial toward "us" and label "them"—
those with whom "we" share the fewest genes and least cul-

ture—as enemies. We have an evolved capacity to see our group as superior to all others and even to be reluctant to recognize members of other groups as deserving of equal respect. A group of the !Kung San of the Kalahari call themselves by a name that literally means "the real people." In their language, the words for "bad" and "foreign" are one and the same. Similarly, the cannibal inhabitants of the delta area of Irian in Indonesian New Guinea call themselves the Asmat, which means "the people—the human beings." All outsiders are known simply as Manowe—"the edible ones."

While far from the realms of cannibalism, I do fear a self-alienation of Christian scholars—many located in rural, isolated communities for the exact historical reason of separation from the alluring temptations of secularism—that reinforces the notion of the secular academy as enemies (whether in theological, political, social, or intellectual terms). There is a depersonalization in such characterizations that exposes a relational arrogance inordinately favoring "us" and disfavoring "them."

We need the relational humility to focus on a personalization of "them"—and them of "us"—that humanizes and decategorizes each other. In so doing, we embrace the pursuit of a greater "us" through which engagement is helped rather than hindered. As I interact with secular colleagues around the fringes of academic engagement at conferences—the meals, the drinks (for which I readily agree to serve as "designated driver" and, immediately, become one of the most popular people at the conference), the excursions to local blues clubs, the cab rides from and to the airport—I find the rich collection of sameness that is too often masked by the overly rigid demarcation of Christian versus secular. I find colleagues who are inordinately proud of their children, have similar hopes, fears, dreams, aspirations, petty jealousies, and insecurities. Perhaps most surprisingly, I find that an increasing number of them wouldn't even describe themselves as "secular"—forcing me to reexamine my assumptions about the validity of "secular" as a descriptor.

Equally important, I challenge their homogenous stereotypes of all Christians as "anti-intellectual," "evangelical," "fundamentalist," or "conservative."[17] My many Jewish colleagues, for instance, within the field of Holocaust and genocide studies, have an opportunity to interact, firsthand, with a Christian who believes resolutely in God's dual covenantal relationship with Jews and with Christians, resulting in a relational space in which I have no interest, nor need, to use our relationship for proselytizing. Through their interaction with me, for all my flaws, they at least see that the Christian world is much more diverse and less predictable on the inside than it looks on the outside, that Christians do not all speak (or shout) in one voice. To the degree this is true, and I think it is, it is a truth only communicated by "us" engaging with "them."

So, at the end of the day, it is this engagement—in a spirit of relational humility—with the secular "other," the feared "them" running throughout much of mainstream Christianity, that may give my voice a hearing in some circles in which it may not be normally heard. It certainly doesn't mean, as I've found out the hard way at times, that I can do second-rate work and have it well-received simply because I have relational connections with secular colleagues at the cutting edge of my disciplinary field. It does mean, though, that if I can rise to the challenge of creating first-rate scholarship informed by a Christian perspective, my chances of having my voice heard in the secular academy are much greater than they would be were I to alienate myself, in a relationally arrogant or fearful manner, from that academy.

WHAT ARE THE RISKS OF THIS MODEL OF ENGAGEMENT?

Some people may see this model of engagement as disingenuous; I'm hiding a significant part of who I am, a Christian, simply to be heard in a world, the secular academy, that might not hear me otherwise. In other words, specifically my mother's, this model doesn't "let my light shine enough" as a Christian. Perhaps one could say that every day I ought to live my life, including my vocation as a teacher-scholar, in ways that clearly say I belong to Christ and that there should be no part of the work I do, or the relationships in which I engage, that does not make it abundantly clear whose I am.

For me, though, the issue is less about other people knowing whose I am (though I certainly go to no great lengths, or any lengths at all, to hide that) and more about what I have to contribute to the secular academy *because* of whose I am. This leads me to conclude that Christian teacher-scholars need be more intentional about finding effective ways to approach that point of engagement—thus, the model I've suggested here as one possible mode.

A more significant risk, to my mind, is that the "Christ the Transformer of Culture" imperative that motivates this model could become "Christ of Culture." So, rather than transforming the secular academy, I may end up accommodating or assimilating Christianity into that academy. In Niebuhr's words, "loyalty to contemporary culture [secular academy] has so far qualified the loyalty to Christ that he has been abandoned in favor of an idol called by his name."[18] In this way, it becomes a theology in our image; what C. S. Lewis called "Christianity And."

This is indeed a risk. It may well be that a model based on humility, particularly a worldview humility some would criticize as too close to religious relativism or universalism (though I think it dangerous to confuse sufficient certainty with absolute uncertainty), makes it likely that I could be "tainted" more by secular ideology or presuppositions than I should be. One of my first published pieces was an article in which I laid out the necessity of Christian institutions to engage culture by fostering value *inoculation* rather than value *indoctrination*.[19] Full of myself, I sent the piece on to one of my mentors from a previous CCCU seminar. He responded with a sentence still written on my heart: "Jim, this is an absolutely first-rate piece of scholarship . . . and is absolutely wrong." His point was that I was too *un*afraid of culture; that I didn't recognize the myriad ways in which engagement with culture may allow culture to work its way into us rather than us working our way into it. So, yes, I have a track record here that drives me to bear in mind the risk that I become seduced by the idols of secular discourse within the academy and lose my authentic Christian voice.

CONCLUSION

This paper has, from a personal perspective, addressed the following question: Who am I called to engage as a scholar and how am I called to engage them? In my own bumbling way, I have tried to explain why it is so important, in my understanding of my vocation as a Christian teacher-scholar, to engage the secular academy. To do so, I have presented a model of engaging the secular academy that revolves around three forms of humility—worldview, intellectual, and relational. Finally, I have tried to be honest about risks of my model of engagement.

Perhaps it's best for me to conclude with at least the appearance of humility I invite others and myself to enact by reiterating that not all Christian teacher-scholars are called to the level of engagement with the secular academy I've described here. Perhaps even more important, those called to such engagement are not necessarily called to proceed in the same manner as I've described my own engagement. For those who, though, are interested in the nitty-gritty of getting into the loaf, I do hope this chapter has at least offered some helpful examples of how that might be done.

NOTES

1. James E. Waller, *Becoming Evil: How Ordinary People Commit Genocide and Mass Killing* (New York: Oxford University Press, 2002, 2nd. ed. 2007).

2. The highest critical acclaim generally comes from family newsletters published by my mother . . . a person who has a track record of being critical of other things I do, so her affirmation is not to be taken lightly.

3. James E. Waller, *Face to Face: The Changing State of Racism Across America* (New York: Perseus Books, 1998).

4. I taught with Mary Stewart Van Leeuwen at a 2002 summer faculty seminar sponsored by CCCU at Wheaton College. I remember two things vividly. First, I recall being awed by the breadth and depth of her intellect. Second, I also recall her warning to me, following my presentation involving the use of evolutionary psychology in my work on perpetrators of genocide, that "those who sup with the devil had better take a long spoon"—an image that kept me away from cutlery of all types for several weeks after and that I still can't get out of my mind.

5. David G. Myers, "Steering Between the Extremes: On Being a Christian Scholar Within Psychology," *Christian Scholars Review 20* (1991): 376-383, quote from p. 383.

6. Nicholas Wolterstorff, "Integration of Faith and Science—The Very Idea," *Journal of Psychology and Christianity* 3 (1984): 12-19, quoted p. 383 in Myers, 1991.

7. While it may be of little interest to you, I find it interesting that, according to Michael Quinion, the origins of "nitty-gritty" are elusive. One explanation is that it is a reduplication—using the same mecha-

nism that has given us *namby-pamby* and *itsy-bitsy*—of the standard English word *gritty*. This has the literal sense of containing or being covered with grit, but figuratively means showing courage and resolve, so the link is plausible, and if it is not the direct origin may have influenced it.

8. H. Richard Niebuhr, *Christ and Culture* (San Francisco: Harper-SanFrancisco, 2001, first published 1951).

9. I am indebted to my insightfully goofy philosopher-friend, Keith Wyma, for the points underlying this summary.

10. For more information about Scholem, see Paul R. Mendes-Flohr's *Gershom Scholem: The Man and His Work* (New York: State University of New York Press, 1994).

11. Niebuhr, *Christ and Culture*, p. 236.

12. Cornel West, *Democracy Matters: Winning the Fight Against Imperialism* (New York: Penguin Books, 2004), pp. 148-149.

13. Ronald Nelson, in *The Reality of Christian Learning: Strategies for Faith-Discipline Integration*, ed. Harold Heie and David L. Wolfe (Grand Rapids, Mich.: Eerdmans, 1987).

14. William Hasker, "Faith-Learning Integration: An Overview," *Christian Scholars Review* 21 (1992): 239.

15. Quoted in Waller, *Becoming Evil* (2nd. ed.), p. 142.

16. Yes, I know—long spoon needed here. But, give it a chance . . . as historians Kari Konkola and Glenn Sunshine conclude, "The hottest field in modern science [evolutionary psychology] is just in the process of discovering the part of human nature which Christianity used to call 'original sin'!" (See p. 159, *Becoming Evil*, 2nd. ed.).

17. A stereotype of Christians which, for me, was broken by the warm, inclusive, and incredibly diverse community of Christian teacher-scholars with whom I had the pleasure to interact at Whitworth University. It was my first year there, when my wife and I attended a James Taylor concert and saw enough faculty present to constitute a quorum for Faculty Assembly, that I knew I was in a "different" place than much of my previous Christian experience. Though I should also say that when colleagues from the History and Theology departments stood up and began to dance to "Steamroller," there was a certain degree of consternation in my mind and heart. Given the hindsight of history, this scene was an unfortunate turn of events that left those of us sitting in Section 122 wishing we were sitting in Section 123.

18. Niebuhr, *Christ and Culture*, p. 110.

19. James E. Waller, "The Case Against Value Indoctrination in Higher Education," *Faculty Dialogue* 19 (1993):65-76.

Chapter 3

Personalism in Politics: Finding Common Ground in the Legislature

Paul DeWeese

Dr. Paul DeWeese received his B.A. from Hope College (Mich.), majoring in philosophy and chemistry. He earned his M.D. from the Wayne State School of Medicine and completed his Residency in Internal Medicine in Grand Rapids, Michigan. He has been Board-Certified in Internal Medicine since 1991.

Dr. DeWeese served two terms, 1999 to 2002, in the Michigan House of Representatives.

My purpose in this essay is to demonstrate the effectiveness of an interpersonal model for discourse in the political arena that focuses on a strategy I used for fostering mutual trust with diverse coalitions to bring about political change. More specifically, I will note the approaches that I, as a Christian, took to develop coalitions across party lines that advanced a public policy agenda I deemed most consistent with my understanding of Christian ethics.

Before presenting a number of case studies from my tenure in the Michigan House of Rrepresentatives, I outline what I mean by "personalism in politics" and my understanding of how such personalism comports with my Christian faith and differs from the expectations of both of our major political parties. I then point to some major temptations faced by Christians doing politics and set the stage for my case studies by describing the cultural and political context for my tenure in Michigan politics. After presenting three case studies, in which I report on how I was able or not able to achieve my political goals. I note mistakes I made along the way and what I would now do differently.

As an elected representative, I understood that my chief duty was to promote "justice" within the proper sphere of responsibility of government. In brief, justice can be viewed broadly as providing "fair treatment" for every person and group of persons in society.[1] Of course, the meaning of "fair" is nuanced and can be debated endlessly. But, we can often intuit when situations are unfair (unjust). In particular, it is not difficult to intuit when the poor, dispossessed, and otherwise marginalized members of our society are not being treated fairly. And the Bible is clear that Christians are called especially to promote justice for "the least of these." But this promotion of justice by government is not directed solely toward the well-being of individuals or select groups. Government should also promote the common good, aspects of well-being that can be shared by all members of society.

This view of government as actively promoting justice is contrary to the common view in our society that government is a necessary evil. That view claims much too little for the vital and beneficial role that government plays in society. I entered politics hoping to be an agent to help unleash government to vigorously promote justice for all citizens. The political strategy I used can most aptly be called "personalism in politics."

PERSONALISM IN POLITICS

By *personalism in politics*, I mean two things. First, such personalism acknowledges the high dignity of the human person, whether she be a member of my political party, a member of another political party, or a member of the public. Second, it means that I engage other persons in a respectful and non-confrontational manner that reflects personal empathy, trying to see and understand things from their perspectives and with genuine concern for their well-being. If we engage others in this way, we will find that our campaign slogans and slick political advertisements do not address the complexities of real life as people experience it.

For example, a campaign slogan of "tax cuts for all" will not help face-to-face discussions with a recently unemployed worker who lost his job to workers in Mexico, and a campaign palm card touting budget cuts will seem grossly irrelevant when looking into the eyes of a mother whose teenage manic-depressive son recently tried to commit suicide because community mental health services have become largely inaccessible. We need to draw close enough to such persons to be able to feel their pain. We cannot truly serve our communities until we are deeply moved by the brokenness of our society and the impact it has on our fellow citizens.

Personalism in politics is also grounded in the reality that each of us is broken and limited in our perspectives and judgments. As Scriptures teaches, we all "see in a mirror, dimly" (1 Cor. 13:12). Therefore, a legislator seeking to do justice must respect the values, skills, and perspectives of legislative colleagues. Personalist politics is not simply a call to be kind and non-confrontational. It includes both the humility necessary to pursue justice in a representative democracy where diverse perspectives flourish and the boldness to cross party lines and join forces with others in the cause of the broad public interest. This will involve getting to know politicians on the other side of the aisle well enough to be able to work collaboratively with them

The case studies that follow illustrate an approach to resolving political gridlock and hyper-partisanship in politics by seeking common ground with those holding to divergent political views. I attempted to implement the "prism of human dignity" as the arbiter of whether a proposal should be supported or opposed. By asking the defining question, Does this proposal enhance or detract from God-endowed human dignity? I found the inspiration to build bridges to members of the other political party based on transcendent norms which supersede the imperatives of blindly supporting my party.

Asking this question does not guarantee that one will arrive at the perfect answer. But it does guarantee that the legislator will have a very different discussion with legislative colleagues than if asking questions commonly posed to resolve an issue: What does our party's governor want? What does the other party's governor want? (Asking either question indicates blind and slavish will to support one's own party at any cost.) What do our party's major donors expect? What do the opinion polls indicate? What is the most effective way to get the public to hold the other party in contempt in order for my party to gain a majority in the next election?

Legislators who eschew the low-minded politics exposed in questions such as these will not have easy or pleasant careers. But, by keeping the concept of human dignity paramount in their minds, they will more likely discover broadly accessible transcendent norms that will enable partnering with legislators holding diverse perspectives.

WHY SHOULD CHRISTIANS DO POLITICS?

Christians are called into political service as a result of their faith commitment. They are not at liberty to pursue their goals according to their own personal priorities because they are in the service of a higher calling, to promote the realization of the kingdom of God. And one aspect of kingdom work is to promote the dignity of human persons, since all persons have been created in the image of God.

Therefore a Christian legislator should work toward the creation of laws that allow the image of God to flourish among all its citizens. This mandate is not derived from the will of the people. Rather, it reflects the nature of God's Creation. As Jim Skillen puts the point, "The normative standards for the just governance of a community of citizens derive from the Creator, not from the people."[2] What motivates the Christian to do politics is the same inspiration that caused God to send Jesus Christ into the world to redeem the world. But we must remember that Jesus did not come simply to redeem individuals but to redeem the entire created order.

When we do politics we enter an arena of public life to serve the world God created and sustains. This is the same world in which God clothed himself in the person of Jesus because he loved it so much. God loves the entire world as it manifests itself in international relations, culture, media, art, politics, business, education, the environment, and economic development. God sustains it all. God dreamed up its majestic possibilities. When we do politics and serve in government, we serve a system that is broken, and, as Scripture puts it, in "bondage to decay" (Rom. 8:21). Yet we believe that by calling on government to serve the claims of justice and the common good, we are fulfilling God's will. Just as God allows the sun to shine on the just and the unjust, so too we are to work for a just political order that serves all people fairly and with equity. Therefore, I believe that Christ's redemptive activity on behalf of the entire created order gives Christians a distinctive and compelling motive for serving in public life.

TEMPTATIONS FOR CHRISTIAN POLITICIANS

Having presented a case for why Christians should do politics, I acknowledge four special temptations that must be carefully avoided.

The first temptation is *the seduction of power.* Power is alluring and beckons us to worship it, because it feeds into our pride, which is the primordial sin. I use the term *worship* here to imply ascribing ultimate worth to power. I also think we consistently underestimate the incredible ability of power to assert itself as an ultimate end and as a means to goals which undermine justice.

A second temptation Christian politicians must strive to overcome is to *give ultimate allegiance to one's political party.* Being conformed to your party as an elected official is a subtle and insidious process, because to serve in the political arena inevitably involves compromise and difficult moral choices. Being a faithful member of one's political party is important. Yet, as C. S. Lewis so poignantly reminds us, "He who surrenders himself without reservation to the temporal claims of a political party is rendering to Caesar that which, of all things, most emphatically belongs to God himself."[3]

A distinctive characteristic of the Christian legislator in the quest for justice is the importance of harnessing the power of the state to protect the poor, the vulnerable, the defenseless, and to ensure that people and systems having power and money do not undermine the rights of such marginalized persons. This is critical because government is often the only effective means of protecting the poor against the calloused greed of the powerful. The following example illustrates the power of money and party allegiance to blind us to the need to protect the poor and vulnerable. A bill was before the Michigan House of Representatives that would have eliminated a thirty percent parking tax on the privately owned parking lots serving Detroit Metro Airport. This tax had been put in place decades before, when the state of Michigan entered into an agreement with Wayne County which gave the county the right to institute the tax to pay for health care for the indigent in the county.

The tax raised $6 million annually. The parking lots, however, had recently come under new owners. They hired a prominent lobbying firm to lobby the legislature to pass the bill eliminating the tax. Our Republican caucus was promised a sizable political contribution, which the owners could well afford due to their envisioned annual $6 million of additional income. (There was nothing in the proposed bill that required that the parking lot rates be reduced.)

The Speaker of the House made it clear that passing this legislation was a high priority for our caucus. But I could not support the bill because no one could tell me how the resources would be replaced to fund indigent health care in Wayne County.

I had worked hard to develop personal relationships with legislators from the Democratic Party. This evolved over time into honest discussions regarding particular bills. These discussions often enabled me to ask questions I hadn't previously thought to ask and to gain perspectives I previously lacked. As I listened to the impact the elimination of funds for indigent health care would have on the real lives of fellow citizens, I came to the conclusion that I could not support the initiative to cut this tax.

Members of my caucus made it clear to me that the political impact of the tax cut for our party was minimal because most of the money was spent in Detroit, which was strongly Democratic, heavily African-American, and largely low-income—groups we did not rely on to maintain out majority. These arguments did not pass the scrutiny that the "prism of human dignity" offered.

As a physician, I had some credibility on this issue and was able to convince enough Republican lawmakers to join the Democrats in opposing this bill. Ultimately enough votes were found to reduce the tax from thirty to twenty-eight percent. This incident taught me a crucial lesson: In the political arena where large amounts of money seek to buy political influence, the rights of the poor and the values of the kingdom of God are easily trampled.

A third temptation that a Christian politician must overcome is to *avoid the moral pretense and spiritual arrogance* that can be significant obstacles to establishing a fully just (and therefore fully Christian) civic order. When we burn with a calling to do justice with kingdom values as our guide, we can easily lose sight of our own moral failings, our blind spots, and our lack of perspective and experience. Although it is exhilarating to stand in the public square and play the prophetic role of speaking God's truths for this generation, Christian legislators must be on guard, lest we sink into moral arrogance by failing to apply God's moral absolutes rightly. As Reinhold Niebuhr puts it,

> Nothing is quite so difficult, yet so genuinely Christian as to remember that in all political struggles there are no saints but only sinners fighting each other. But the Christian faith gives him no warrant to lift himself above the world's perplexities and to seek to claim absolute validity for the stand he takes. It does, instead, encourage him to charity which is born of humility and contrition.[4]

The fourth temptation a Christian politician must avoid is to *compel a type of spiritual ideology on all of society.* It is not the role of Christians to impose our version of Rabbinic law or Shariah law but rather to contend for unbiased justice for all. Jim Skillen persuasively argues that "the political community exists to uphold public justice for all."[5] That quest must include doing justice to all, including those who serve idols and deny their ultimate obligation to God.

It is not government's mandate to coerce behavior consistent with any sectarian system of beliefs. Rather, the role of government is to establish and sustain public justice for everyone under its authority. Therefore, Christians must appeal to norms of justice that are universal when attempting to be persuasive in the public square. We argue best on the basis of moral discernment shared by all persons by virtue of all humans being created in God's image.

THE CULTURAL AND POLITICAL
CONTEXT FOR MY POLITICAL TENURE

To create a framework that will enable understanding my later case studies of how I attempted to build diverse coalitions to promote justice, I will now reflect on the cultural and political context for my tenure in the Michigan House of Representatives.

Politics, although rooted in the acquisition and use of power, fulfills its legitimate function when it serves the claims of justice. But too often politics disregards the claims of justice and supinely serves the claims of special interests bought with money and motivated by greed. A crisis of our contemporary age is that we have fundamentally perverted the governing process. Instead of engaging in politics to secure the right to govern in the broad public interest, we subvert the process of governing and usurp it on behalf of keeping a particular party in control. We don't so much engage in politics to secure the privilege of governing on behalf of all citizens equitably as we use the reigns and resources of government primarily either to perpetuate a political party's current majority and power or to gain a party's majority in the next election.

Christians must be a counter-cultural force in this degraded process. We must answer "In whose interest do we govern?" differently than many of our colleagues.

In this context, the existence of term limits for Michigan legislators presents a significant problem. Money becomes of paramount importance when there are term limits. Without term limits, legislators have the time to establish a strongly grounded reputation. Thy have good name recognition in the communities they represent. They generally do not need to raise money, and, therefore, are less dependent on their caucus for financial support.

In contrast, legislators with term limits do not have sufficient opportunity to become well known in one or two terms and so must secure the large amounts of money it takes to buy name recognition. As a result, since term limits have become law in

Michigan, the political process has moved from being focused outward on governing wisely toward being focused inward on political control of the governing process.

As this phenomenon has grown, caucus leaders expect a legislator's primary allegiance to be directed toward the success of the caucus. There is a diminished patience and acceptance of politicians who vote their conscience, because this decreases the capacity of caucus leaders to deliver votes on behalf of influential political investors. Caucus leaders know that these "investors" will quickly take their money elsewhere if they cannot rely on a predictable process for securing their private goals.

Is it any wonder, then, that our society now largely sees government as an evil, tax-sucking, bureaucratic monster? In this view, there is little room for thinking of government as a positive good—as an effective means for enhancing human dignity and fostering justice.

How our society treats its citizens, especially the poor, refugees, the disabled, the mentally ill, and the aged, directly affects the welfare of all of us. It sustains or corrodes our collective soul. I am not talking here of providing food stamps so the hungry won't rob our homes. Rather, how we do justice (or injustice) either evokes a sense of shared responsibility for the welfare of others—or caters to our most contemptible instincts for greed.

In short, our citizens and our political culture have largely lost a commitment to justice. We no longer believe our politics ought to create a consensus that is fair to those who are most vulnerable and all other members of our society. In this view, private action is considered most virtuous. When the poor are locked out of political consideration, this view justifies itself by claiming that the poor will adapt in their desperate attempts to cope and through their struggles will be better equipped to support themselves. This radically individualistic view holds that each person rightly rises or falls on his or her own merits. In this view, when government is sufficiently limited, the marketplace will by itself produce private virtue through disciplining our habits.

What saddened me most about this political environment during my years in Lansing was the co-optation of the evangelical Christian community by the economically conservative ideological and business interests. As a result, the evangelical community, which was awakened from its political slumber in the 1980s, had been joined at the hip with economic interests that undermine the very biblical worldview to which evangelicals claim to give allegiance. The well-intentioned convictions of evangelicals have been cynically exploited by those who already have wealth and power and don't want government to diminish their largesse in any way on behalf of justice. Such evangelicals need to hear again the voice of Jesus, warning his followers about losing their prophetic voice: "You are the salt of the earth, but if the salt has lost its taste, how can its saltiness be restored? It is no longer good for anything, but it is thrown out and trampled under foot" (Matt. 5:13).

OVERVIEW OF CASE STUDIES

The three case studies that follow illustrate an approach to resolving political gridlock and hyper-partisanship in the political arena and fostering political stewardship by seeking common ground among persons who hold diverse political commitments. I set out to create both political and interpersonal transformation through relationship building. At the heart of the process was listening to other views and judging their merit on the criterion of whether they enhanced human dignity rather than enhancing the power of one caucus over the other. Once others came to trust that my highest allegiance was not to my caucus but to promoting human dignity and justice, it enabled the development of partnerships and coalitions committed to a common political agenda. At the same time, it confounded the political establishment that has come to value and expect political conformity. This led to resistance, and, at times, overt hostility from my own caucus and party.

CASE STUDY 1: BUILDING RELATIONSHIPS
WITH THE AFRICAN-AMERICAN COMMUNITY

My first case study focuses on building relationships outside of the legislative arena. Because of my community involvement, I frequently worked alongside African-American clergy in Lansing, Michigan's capitol. I began to worship with their congregations on Sundays. I made a commitment to listen, to understand their perspectives on the issues that were important to their communities. As I listened, I came to understand better the ways in which I benefited from "white privilege"—that complex social matrix within which I am treated differently than persons of color relative to barriers to opportunity based on judgments about race.

An example of the reality of how racial prejudice operates to undermine opportunity occurred in my legislative office. On being elected, I offered a job to a well-qualified African-American. My senior staff told me I shouldn't hire him because I represented Howell and Cohoctah Township, which was the home of the former Grand Knight of the Ku Klux Klan. I was told that if I hired him, I might not be re-elected. I offered him the job anyway, but this incident helped me to understand that racial barriers are still present in our society.

During my first term in office, I brought the Union Missionary Baptist Church choir, composed primarily of African-Americans, to the Court House in Howell, Michigan, for a celebration of the birthday of Dr. Martin Luther King Jr. This initiative served to communicate to my constituents that I would not countenance racial prejudice, and it also demonstrated to the black community that I was not afraid to use my office to promote racial reconciliation.

As I got to know the black community through building these relationships, I began to understand better the actual experiences of African-Americans. I became convinced that the black community did not desire to be dependent on government programs, such as welfare. Rather, they were looking for ways to decrease the remaining barriers to social mobility and equal opportunity. I began to speak out about the profound racial disparities in both access to health care and health outcomes. For example, in Michigan, African-Americans are seven times more likely to become blind from glaucoma than are whites. Black men die from prostate cancer at twice the rate of white men, and the difference between black and white maternal mortality is larger in Michigan than in any other state.

During my first term, I was selected to chair a House Republican Task Force on Access to Health Care. The expectation was that we would come up with various tax reduction strategies to incentivize businesses to offer health coverage to their employees. While the report of our task force did recommend such strategies, it also graphically highlighted the profound disparities in access to health care that African-Americans face in Michigan. The task force report was buried by the speaker of the House, who did not allow it to be distributed to the public. I was told that highlighting racial disparities might be embarrassing to our party and could give the Democrats a tool to criticize our party before the next election. I was saddened by this reaction, because I was convinced that if my party honestly addressed the real issue confronting the African-American community, we would have a chance to build bridges of understanding that would both change our party's policies and, potentially, earn the support of more African-Americans on election day.

I also worked with the African-American community to create church-based after-school programs where children could receive tutoring and learn computer skills. I worked to allow the hundreds of used state computers sitting in government warehouses to be donated to these church centers, so that when the children learned to use a computer, they would be given a free computer as a reward. This could reduce the "digital divide" so prevalent in urban centers.

Due to efforts to understand the African-American community and use the influence of my office to to address their concerns, I was able to secure significant open and active political support from this community. The senior pastor of one of the more influential black churches in my district, and chair of the Council of Black Pastors in Lansing, chaired my campaign for the State Senate. The political community was confounded when fourteen influential black pastors held a press conference to endorse my candidacy. My ability to gain the support of our city's black pastors reflected my longstanding commitment to racial reconciliation. Earlier in my political career, I was also the first white Republican ever to seek and receive the endorsement of the Council of Baptist Pastors in Detroit when I ran for the State House of Representatives in a rural, largely white district.

CASE STUDY 2: HONORING STATE WORKERS

My second case study involves a bipartisan effort that I led to honor state employees. As the ideology is propagated that government is, by its very nature, unproductive, state employees are cast in a negative light. I came to believe that our public discourse is impoverished and the public square sullied when our citizens are fed a continual diet that says the government is our enemy, inherently incapable of doing anything good. To the extent that the purpose of government and its capacity to make society better is denigrated, the body politic has nowhere to go to address the critical issues affecting all of us.

The government is one place where the public interest is carried out. It is the provider of services that cannot be provided by the private sector. Among other initiatives, it creates laws that define fair economic practice, that help to protect our environment, that ensure our food is safe, and that uphold our civil rights. For example, when hepatitis infected our strawberry crop in Michigan, my constituents wanted to know what the Department of Community Health would do to protect them. When tuberculosis threatened to ravage our cattle, the devotees of the private sector suddenly turned to the Department of Agriculture for action. And when we had potholes in our roads, the public turned to the Department of Transportation.

I found out that the mentality of constantly denigrating the role of government in helping to create decent and livable communities has a powerful effect on how we treat state employees. If the entire enterprise of state government is suspect, then the workers who faithfully carry out its obligations are seen as less than respectable. As a result, it is not unusual to treat them with contempt and disrespect.

In that context, I initiated a State Worker Appreciation Day to further three distinct but compatible goals. First, I wanted to educate the broader public about the vital role that government plays every day in our lives to create decent, livable communities. I also wanted to counter the corrosive message that government is but a burden and largely unnecessary. Finally, I wanted to honor the outstanding work generally performed every day by state workers.

I worked with Democratic lawmakers to create a yearly event on the front lawn of the Capitol building, during which we provided a free lunch to state employees. We established the Camelot awards to honor workers who had demonstrated exemplary service on behalf of the public good.

About 2,400 state workers attended the first of these annual events, as did over 6,000 two years later. State workers flooded the lawn of the capitol, eager to hear someone honor their hard work. I believe the State Worker Appreciation Day helped to create a new understanding and appreciation for the outstanding service that state workers perform on behalf of the public good and a new public dialogue about their indispensable role. It also began to promote the important message that we cannot build a decent society unless our public institutions are respected and strong enough to adequately foster the public interest and promote public justice.

CASE STUDY 3: FURTHER
INITIATIVES TO FOSTER RACIAL RECONCILIATION

My good experience building caring personal relationships with the African-American community, as reported on in my first case study, led me to take further initiatives to foster racial reconciliation. Because of my relationships with the African-American community and especially African-American legislators, I was coming to a fuller realization of the profound impact that state-sanctioned racial discrimination had on our society. I believe deeply that God has created all persons in his image and that Christ is reconciling all people to himself through his death and resurrection. Yet it became painfully clear to me that our society has developed a pattern of laws and practices that still discriminate against people of color (despite the progress in race relations that had been made since the 1960s). Whether one looks at the inadequate way the Public Defenders program represents the poor, or the great disparities in access to health care for people of color compared to whites, or the inadequate opportunities for Hispanic and black children to access quality educations and the catastrophic impact this has on their social mobility and the opportunity to fulfill their God-given potential, one simply cannot defend the status quo as acceptable.

Despite this, the economically and socially conservative community vigorously claims that government has no role in addressing these disparities. For them, any initiatives to redress inequalities only represent big government. But, the black community continues to hope that government will be honest about the social and economic problems facing them. They would like government to take the initiative to remove the remaining barriers that undermine the opportunity for equal opportunity for all. The argument that government has no business addressing these issues is a sad reminder to the black community of the arguments once used to delay passage of the Voting Rights Act and other civil rights legislation.

I believe that if a dialogue could be established through which legislators came together to learn from one another, then our legislature as a whole might be willing to do more to be proactive relative to the critical issues facing the black community. Let me report on one such legislative attempt.

Representative Buzz Thomas from Detroit and I co-chaired a dialogue on racial reconciliation. We hosted a number of dinners and brought in an experienced mediator form Detroit to help the dialogue. These discussions were helpful in deepening our understanding of the issues. Although I had hoped that bipartisan legislation would be generated as a result of this initiative, that was not to be. Rather, it was made clear to me that by highlighting this kind of across-the-aisle cooperation, we would make it more difficult to sharpen the differences between the two parties at the next election. If, because of our coalition building, we couldn't make the Democrats out to be the enemy, it would make it more difficult to convince the voting public of the need to maintain or strengthen our majority come election time.

During this time, the governor proposed that the state of Michigan take over the Detroit public school system because it was failing to deliver a quality education for too many students. This proposal immediately created a passionate and intense outcry form the citizens of Detroit and their legislators. The proposal would have eliminated the Detroit school board and thus the capacity of Detroit's largely black electorate to vote for people to represent them. This resurrected painful memories of a racist past when a white power structure denied blacks the right to vote.

As the debate that the governor's proposal generated became more heated, state representative Kwame Kilpatrick, later to become Detroit's mayor (before scandal forced his resignation), asked me if I would spend a day with him in Detroit to see if we could fashion an acceptable alternative to the governor's proposal that would both fundamentally restructure Detroit public schools and maintain the right of the citizens of Detroit to elect their school board. Believing it essential to both deliver a better education to Detroit's children and to respect the voters of the city, we developed an outline of an alternative plan to radically restructure the Detroit system and retain the voting rights of its citizens.

Despite our best efforts, we were unable to prevail. Although I was a member of the Education Committee, I was not even able to persuade the committee chair to bring up our proposal for discussion. I was told that since the governor's prestige was on the line, it was our duty to pass his proposal without even considering alternatives. The governor's proposal passed.

The legislation that passed contained a provision that gave the citizens of Detroit the opportunity to vote whether to retain the state takeover or return to the traditional form of school governance after five years. When the five years were up, Detroit's citizens voted by a large majority to eliminate the state takeover—a vote largely motivated by anger caused by the legislation's elimination of the right to elect their own school board. The tragedy of the failure to consider an alternative to the governor's plan is highlighted by the fact that Detroit's public schools currently have the largest drop-out rate of any major city in the country (greater than seventy percent).

Mistakes Along the Way

I have told my story of how I tried to make a difference as a politician by rising above the debilitating parochialism of slavishly following party, by developing personal relationships of trust with elected officials across the divide of political partisanship and race, and by applying the transcendent criterion of promoting human dignity as the guidepost for whether a policy should be supported. In pursuit of my policy goals, I sometimes encountered hostility and antagonism within my own party. But it is also important for me to acknowledge that part of the reason I ran into obstacles was my own failings. In this chapter, I have argued that the way we typically do politics is deeply flawed. Yet my experience demonstrated my own shortcomings. I will now share some of the mistakes I made, pointing to how I would do some things differently if I ever serve in public office again.

Although I was passionate about pursuing public justice, I was not always effective. My passion led me to succumb to the fourth temptation noted above, coming across as judgmental and arrogant. An example of this occurred when the legislature engineered a $22,000 pay raise for its members. I felt this was a terrible injustice, since we were, at the same time, cutting programs in many areas and the economy was suffering. This pay raise created a sense of revulsion and outrage among our constituents. I felt this action was self-serving. It buttressed the image of elected officials serving themselves first. I also felt this action undermined the trust necessary for our system of government to work well.

Because of these deep convictions, I chose to give my pay raise to the community, and I went public with my decision. This created media attention, and as I spoke my mind, my words were interpreted as being critical of my colleagues. By giving back my raise with such righteous indignation, I cast my colleagues in a selfish light. As a public person, I felt compelled to act publicly. I could have accomplished my purpose with greater circumspection.

Another way in which I exercised poor judgment was through my propensity to air too freely my disagreements with the governor or my party. I was aware of how the public felt about politicians who frequently cover up the truth and speak out of both sides of their mouths. I was committed to a different, more authentic course. Yet at times I unnecessarily antagonized members of my caucus, the governor, and my party. Unless elected officials limit the number of issues on which they publicly disagree with their caucus, they are soon seen as unreliable and perhaps even untrustworthy. You can, at times, disagree with your caucus and still retain their good graces. But you must choose your battles. Politics involves tough compromises. A person cannot fight every battle, at least not openly in the press. Being a member of a caucus does create legitimate expectations of being committed to the success of the caucus as a group.

I also made the mistake of trying to accomplish too many things at once. Governor Engler gave me some good advice that I too often failed to apply in practice. He told me I could accomplish almost anything I wanted as a legislator, but I could not accomplish everything I wanted. To be more effective, I should have focused my energies around a few goals. To be a good legislator, one must balance fervor and passion with prudence, patience, and restraint.

CONCLUSION

I believe politics is a noble calling. It can be a means for loving God with all our heart, soul, mind, and strength. The way we govern ourselves is a testimony to our ideals and a test of our character as a people. Properly seen, government represents our commitment to all of us. It is a vital channel through which to provide a legacy worthy of our people and of our children.

Each generation of citizens benefit greatly from legislators who are tenaciously committed to doing justice. These men and women are transformational leaders, and they understand that the task is not so much to see what no one has yet seen, but to think new thoughts and ask new questions about that which everyone sees. What characterizes them in their legislative work is that they do the following:

- place principles above politics;
- recognize the importance of fidelity to transcendent norms, as opposed to being willing to change core positions based on public opinion;
- are statespersons committed to the well-being of present and future generations, as opposed to being politicians committed only to winning the next election;
- call people together around a vision of "we the people," as opposed to pandering to our selfishness;
- emphasize our obligations and responsibilities, as opposed to catering to our entitlements and wants;
- are willing to embrace good ideas that originate from other political parties, rather than denouncing an idea simply because it came from the other side of the political divide;
- are more interested in creating a healthy society and being good stewards of a government that serves real people than in securing a shallow and temporary victory for a political party.

NOTES

1. For a very accessible elaboration on the meaning of "justice," see Steve Monsma, *Healing for a Broken World: Christian Perspectives on Public Policy* (Wheaton, Ill.: Crossway Books, 2008), pp. 46-61.

2. Private conversation in January 2008.

3. C. S. Lewis, *The Weight of Glory* (New York, Harper Collins Publishers, 1949), p. 53.

4. From "Reinhold Niebuhr in Politics," excerpted in *Reinhold Niebuhr, Theologian of Public Life*, ed. Larry Rasmussen (Philadelphia: Fortress Press, 1991), p. 130.

5. Private conversation, January 2008.

Chapter 4

Fostering Environmental Responsibility Among Watermen of Chesapeake Bay: A Faith and Action Research Approach

Susan Drake Emmerich

Susan Drake Emmerich is currently the CEO of Emmerich Environmental Consulting and director of the Creation Care Program for the Center for Law and Culture. She is a former professor of Environmental Science at Trinity Christian College. Emmerich also was the founder and former Executive Director of the Tangier Watermen's Stewardship for the Chesapeake (TaSC), a non-profit organization formed to implement the Tangier Watermen's Stewardship 2020 Vision Plan. She received her Ph.D. in 2003 from the Gaylord Nelson Institute of Environmental Studies at the University of Wisconsin, Madison, under the direction of Professor Calvin B. DeWitt.

She is the co-producer of the 2007 Redemptive Film Award-winning documentary entitled *When Heaven Meets Earth: Faith and the Environment in the Chesapeake Bay*. She is also the co-producer of the 2007 documentary entitled *When Heaven Meets Earth: Faith-*

based *Stewardship Spreads to the Urban and Suburban Communities* which chronicles her latest stewardship work among the African-American community of Berlin, Maryland. Her action and faith-based stewardship research work is also the subject of the Telly and Aurora Award winning PBS documentary on the Tangier Watermen's Initiative entitled *Between Heaven and Earth: The Plight of the Chesapeake Bay Watermen.*

Emmerich also spent ten years in the federal government. As a former U.S. Delegate to the UN and U.S. negotiator for the Department of State, she was a key negotiator at the 1992 Earth Summit, Biological Diversity Convention, Global Climate Convention, and the Chair of the Secretariat for the International Coral Reef Initiative. She worked on environmental issues for the U.S. Senate Foreign Relations Committee, the World Bank, EPA, and Department of Interior as a Presidential Management Fellow. Dr. Emmerich also served as the Director of the East Coast office of the Au Sable Institute of Environmental Studies, a Christian environmental educational organization, and as Vice-President of the Au Sable Institute's Board of Directors.

Nobel Laureate Henry Kendall claims that "Environmental problems at their root are human, not scientific or technical." He is right. Neither environmental professionals nor academics can hope to solve environmental problems with an approach that simply addresses a particular scientific or technical issue absent the human context in which these issues exist. Public policy professionals and scholars need to generate approaches to environmental problems with and for the people directly involved and within the relational context of peoples' community and culture. However, *many academics, policymakers, environmentalists, and scientists maintain the authority of modern technocratic science, and this monopolizes the definition of knowledge. Those holding this worldview, certain of its successful achievements in manipulating the physical environment,* often without intention *devalue the ideas, experiences, and accumulated wisdom of those who* would foster holistic solutions to environmental problems.[1]

The case study of the watermen of Tangier Island in the Chesapeake Bay clearly illustrates the truth of the above claim. Over the past decade, many have warned that prevailing societal patterns seriously threaten the planet. This is the case with the watermen of the Chesapeake Bay. Human-made pollution from cities, farms, and fisheries; microbial disease; and over-harvesting of fisheries has left only one fishery—the blue crab—as the basis for the waterman's economy. The specific human problem is the social conflict between the Chesapeake Bay Foundation (CBF) environmentalists and the resource dependent and faith-based waterman[2] community of Tangier Island over how to deal with the pollution of the Bay and island, the decline of the fisheries, and limiting harvest of oysters and blue crabs.

This case study prompts two questions. *Could faith-based stewardship provide a framework for the Tangier people to willingly change their practices to better steward the fishery and the island environment and plan for their economy's sustainability?* And, could *faith-based stewardship foster a better relationship between the Tangier community and the environmentalists.*[3]

THE CONTEXT AND PROBLEM

In 1997 I conducted my Ph.D. research among an isolated Christian watermen community in the Virginia waters of the Chesapeake Bay called Tangier Island.

Tangier is a marshy island only 3.4 miles long and 1.5 miles wide, an hour by boat from the mainland of Maryland and just over three hours from Washington D.C. Its people are known to cling tenaciously to cherished traditions, conventional folk wisdom, and the motto, *"simper eadem, always the same."*[4] Tangier's economy centers almost entirely on the harvesting of blue crabs. The two churches on the island are the center of community life as it was 200 years ago. Of the 700 inhabitants, eighty-four percentconsider themselves conservative, evangelical Christians.

Conflict over the fisheries has been a part of Tangier's history dating back to the oyster wars in the mid-to late-1800s. Now, fishery conflicts ensue over oyster and Blue Crab regulations set by state boards of fisheries. In Virginia regulations are set by the Virginia Marine Resources Commission, and influenced by proposals from environmental groups such as the Chesapeake Bay Foundation (CBF), whose motto is "Save the Bay?" In 1995, conflict erupted on Smith and Tangier Islands over a blue crab regulation proposed by CBF that would have created a crab sanctuary and put watermen out of work for the winter. Irate watermen placed signs against CBF on their crab shanties and along island channels. It also led to violence on Smith Island when a CBF shed was burned. I went to Tangier to better understand the causes of the conflict between CBF and the Tangier islanders, and to see if a faith-based approach to stewardship could provide a bridge to the two groups working together to help save the fishery and the culture of the watermen.

GOALS FOR THE RESEARCH

The research encompassed three basic goals: (1) to expose academics, scientists, government officials, and environmentalists to the important role of faith in the way people view the world and solve community problems; (2) to transform individuals' ways of thinking and acting for the benefit of the Tangiermen's community, economy, and island and Bay environment; and (3) to promote peaceful working relations between the Chesapeake Bay Foundation and the Tangier watermen for the benefit of the blue crab fishery and the Chesapeake Bay.

My hope was that this case might be a landmark effort to help environmentalists and scientists understand better how faith can be a motivating force for changing people's views and behaviors toward the environment, environmentalists, and economic sustainability. I employed, therefore, a unique interpersonal model of engagement based on a research design employing a mix of research and education methods that gave a voice to the people and allowed for a multifaceted and participatory role for the researcher.

RESEARCH DESIGN

To implement the model of engagement, the challenge was to understand first the causes for the conflict and what role, if any, the Tangiermen's faith could have in resolving that conflict. I based my research design, therefore, on a "participatory paradigm" *that provides the conditions for personal and social transformation that redresses injustices, supports peace, and forms spaces for democracy and ecological harmony.*[5] It also allows the researcher *to participate with the community in the generation of new knowledge for their benefit, and the benefit of the academic community.*[6]

I conducted two phases of research using a mix of ethnography and action research. I chose ethnography because it is a research method directed at giving a voice to others by giving the researcher a means to discover and understand people's unique history and views about their world. I chose action research because it put the problem solving process in control of the local people based on their worldview and enabled me, as the researcher, to help the community toward an improved environmental, economic, and social situation.

Before embarking on the ethnography, I conducted several months of preliminary research on the regional and communal context in which watermen live and work and the relationship between watermen and scientists. I read many books on the history of the Methodist church in the region and its influences, the political and economic history of the region and the islands, and the psychological make-up of fishermen, islanders, and their blood cousins the Appalachian mountain people.

From this information, I developed a "cultural portrait" of the people and their relationship to the environment that revealed ways in which people, historically and presently, reacted to change, conflict, and outsiders, and interacted with their environment. Moreover, I identified the key human, social, and political forces for change in the community. This ethnographic research provided vital information in determining successful ways to institute change on the island.

INTERPERSONAL ETHNOGRAPHY

I conducted the ethnography under a participatory paradigm that allows the researcher to be more interpersonal and relational rather than impersonal and detached. Many scientists and social scientists believe incorrectly that being detached from the subjects is the only way to achieve an accurate representation of the reality of the situation. However, early in my research I identified regional "consultants," a group of people I contacted throughout my project who provided an outsider's view of the people and their culture. With their help, I maintained the validity of interview data and untangled varying accounts of the conflict while developing genuine relationships with the people I was interviewing.

To gain community acceptance and ownership of the research, I began with the "gatekeepers" of the Tangier community's worldview—the church and its leaders. I sought first the approval of Tangier Methodist church's board of directors that included the assistant pastor, also mayor of Tangier. I submitted a letter to the board explaining my background and the purpose for the research and a pastoral letter of reference. The board recognized that the research would benefit their citizens by providing a new understanding of Scripture related to the fishery and the Bay and by enabling them to have a greater voice in fishery policy. Hence, they saw me both as a researcher and as a messenger or, in their faith language, a missionary to their island.

The Virginia Waterman's Representative to the state board of fisheries first introduced me to the leaders among the Tangier Island watermen. His introduction provided me some credibility with watermen. I chose to live at the same economic level as the majority of the islanders to comprehend better their way of life and economic hardships. Moreover, I participated in church by attending worship services, teaching Sunday school, and reading the Scriptures from the pulpit at services. My religious participation was not contrived but normal practice in my own life and one of the more important aspects of developing relationships, trust, and credibility among the faith community.

I often assisted the women in the processing of crabs. In addition, I dressed according to island's conservative standards and asked permission from watermen's wives to conduct interviews with their husbands. More importantly, my residence was with a Tangier widow, my age, and her two children. Through her introductions, I developed genuine relationships with many islanders.

Many factors contributed to my ability to garner trust in a short time and to work with the people on an equal level. First, members and leaders of the Methodist church and a respected waterman representative formally introduced me to islanders.

Second, the Methodist church leaders and the mayor of Tangier accepted the research and me as a messenger.

Third, most in the community understood that my sincere desire was to serve the Tangier citizens and people of the region through my research.

Fourth, I built lasting relationships among people on both sides of the conflict; relationships that still last to this day.

Fifth, I respected Tangier's cultural mores and taboos by living according to them, including participating fully in the life of the Methodist church.

Sixth, I lived with a Tangier family at the same economic level as the majority of islanders.

Last, but certainly not least, I listened and incorporated people's ideas and views into every step of the ethnographic process.

Environmental or other public policy projects that have as a central goal to promote social change of any sort can benefit greatly from ethnographic research conducted in a similar manner. An approach in which the change agent or researcher sincerely develops relationships and genuinely seeks people's views in a manner sensitive to their cultural values and worldview will undoubtedly serve well the social and environmental change goals of any public policy and environmental practitioner.

Ethnographic Understanding of People and Conflict

After six months of research, the ethnography revealed that the Tangier women, pastors, and lay church leaders were important change agents on the island and the church was the most powerful institutional force for change. It also showed that the biblical ethic of stewarding God's creation provided the Tangiermen with the basis for "living right" with the environment. Many environmentalists had operated on the assumption that the Tangiermen not only did not have an environmental ethic but that their faith was the greatest hindrance to their acceptance of an environmental stewardship message. In fact, it never occurred to most of the CBF staff that faith provided any meaning or had any influence over the way the Tangiermen viewed the world let alone the Chesapeake Bay. As a result, the Tangiermen did not accept the environmentalist's particular stewardship message because the environmentalists had not won the "right to be heard." Some CBF staff did not take time to understand the Tangiermen's faith worldview nor to speak in terms understood within that worldview. Many of the environmentalists did not respect the island's cultural values. Their educational staff, some of whom were young college students, drank, partied, and smoked and did not participate in the life of the church. This led the Tangiermen to be suspicious of the environmentalists' motivations for being on the island and wary of their message.

Mistrust was the single most important cause of the conflict between the Tangier people and CBF. This mistrust stemmed from two factors. First, the Tangiermen feared losing their livelihood and way of life. The Tangiermen felt powerless to control fishery regulations and the steady decline of the fishery. Their inability to control their situation fueled conflicts with outsiders they perceived as threatening their livelihoods. Second, the conflict stemmed from the differences in worldview and language between the two groups. Watermen rely on experiential and historical knowledge and speak about the fishery within that context. Most environmentalists use a scientific approach and express themselves using technical and mathematical language. The two groups talked past each other, each not listening or understanding the other or sometimes, not respecting their neighbor's worldview. This led to frustration, misperceptions, and mistrust.

STEWARDSHIP ETHIC: A BRIDGE FOR MUTUAL UNDERSTANDING

Despite the mistrust and worldview and language differences, the common goal bridging the gap between the watermen and CBF was a mutual value—the desire for clean islands and a healthy Chesapeake Bay fishery. My hypothesis was that the combination of a mutual understanding of environmental stewardship and respect for each other's worldview could be key factors that would help ameliorate the conflict between the two groups. The challenge was to enable CBF officials and staff to more fully appreciate and respect the Tangiermen's cultural values, faith-based worldview, and knowledge base in hope that it could lead to a working relationship between the two parties in support of environmental stewardship. Among the Tangiermen, the challenge was threefold: (1) to elucidate the biblical worldview as it relates to the created order, their neighbors, and obedience to civil laws, and for them to take account of the way in which they did or did not live up to this biblical worldview; (2) to awaken the island residents from their malaise and inspire them to make a difference in their community's present and future environment and economy; and (3) to help them in establishing the organizational means to implement constructive change.

FAITH-BASED STEWARDSHIP AND ACTION
RESEARCH APPROACH TO INSTITUTING SOCIAL CHANGE

At the Tangier Mayor's request, I returned to the island to work with people to develop a faith-based stewardship initiative led by Tangiermen. I implemented an approach to institute constructive change based on seven principles derived from the ethnographic studies of the people (cultural portrait), the conflict, and the political and social forces for instituting change in the community. First, the Tangier people were placed in a position of control and leadership. Second, the people were the generators and implementers of ideas. The Tangiermen already had ideas about ways to solve the problems they faced; they simply needed a channel through which to express them and an audience to listen. Third, I based the approach on their faith worldview and its source of authority, the Bible. Their faith was the lens through which they understood the world and the paradigm from which they operated. In addition, their faith had served, historically, as an important mediating force against feelings of powerlessness, enabling some to rise above adversity and institute necessary change for the benefit of the community.

Fourth, the approach involved the churches as the institutional framework and support with the pastors and laity in leadership roles. Fifth, as the implementers of change in the community, the Tangier women were part of the leadership. Sixth, I used a shared-praxis approach to education, a process of transformational change through critical reflection, reevaluation, reinterpretation, and re-habituation. This educational approach helped the women and watermen to see the dissonance between their own beliefs and practices and resolve the dissonance. Critical reflection occurred through various forums and means such as environmental stewardship sermons that employed creation hymns and religious pictures of Jesus in creation. In addition, it occurred through Bible studies on creation stewardship, community meetings, and one-on-one discussions. Last, the approach incorporated co-generated learning in which the re-searcher and community collaboratively problem-solved. Co-generated learning took place in community meetings and in newly formed community groups called Families Actively In-volved in Tangier's Heritage (FAIITH) and the Tangier Water-men's Stewardship for the Chesapeake (TaSC).

ROLE OF THE RESEARCHER

My role as a researcher changed from being a participant ob-server while conducting the ethnograph to being a co-researcher and co-worker with members of the community during the ac-tion-research or faith-based stewardship initiative phase. The multifaceted and participatory role as an action researcher was an important component of the interpersonal model of engage-ment. At any given time, I was in one or several of the following positions: encourager, educator or messenger, and peacemaker who legitimized, sustained, and advocated. Central to all these positions was the role of a *paraclete*. The Greek translation of the word *paraclete* is "called alongside of." Translations of *paraklesis* are "exhortation, encouragement, and comfort." It also means "helper, advocate, or pleader." To help the Tangiermen move toward an environmentally and economically sustainable fu-ture, I, as the researcher, "walked alongside of" the people for a time.

In this capacity, I reflected back to the local group things about themselves or habits that (1) were not consistent with their faith worldview and did not accurately reflect concern for their fishery or environment; (2) would not be a productive way to ap-proach discussions with people outside the community; or (3) would hinder them from reaching their goals. I did not shy away from naming certain behavior as wrong, such as breaking civil laws, particularly fishery laws. Overall, through pulpit mes-sages, Bible studies, and church and community meetings, I at-tempted to fill in pieces of their faith-based worldview with bib-lical principles that addressed economic, financial, and environ-mental stewardship.

Throughout the action research or stewardship initiative, I *encouraged* people to realize the valuable knowledge they al-ready had to solve their community problems. I encouraged them to take risks and to institute beneficial changes. In addition, I assisted people in constructive conflict, discouraged destructive conflict, and provided support in times of disappointment, discouragement, and ostracization. I also helped the creation of the 2020 Vision by ensuring the consideration of every voice and idea in the community meetings along with encouraging people to think biblically and creatively—"beyond the box" and "out of their comfort zone." Moreover, it was critical to help people think of the three R's: reduce, reuse, and recycle when developing community stewardship goals.

The most important role was that of *educator or messenger*. I presented new information and helped participants reflect critically on their present actions in light of the new knowledge. I provided cases of successful attempts by other fishing communities to institute economic and regulatory change, and I brought to the island outsiders from other watermen communities to share their experiences in addressing fishery issues in the political arena. Teaching and sharing information better enabled the Tangier citizens to discuss issues with the forces of power. I also helped people inventory and assess the local resources available in their community to implement the effort. In addition, I provided scientific, economic, governmental, and environmental information from outside sources and guidance on how to read and analyze the documents. Moreover, I revealed how to work with people from outside institutions such as government and how to apply democratic approaches to civic governance. I encouraged people to reflect on instances in their own history of how they accomplished projects with non-island groups.

My goals as a peacemaker were to elicit peaceful settlement and cooperation, making it a more attractive option than coercion or violence; to attend to issues of justice; to stand with the disputing parties in working through their conflict; and to enable the parties to deal constructively with future conflict. As a peacemaker, I did not make peace but helped create the conditions that allowed the disputing parties to choose peace and reconciliation. To help the right choice, I found myself being, at times, a *legitimizer*, one who tries to help establish the credibility of the weaker party's needs in the eyes of the skeptical stronger party. I encouraged outside professionals such as governmental officials, environmentalists, and scientists to recognize, respect, and incorporate the waterman's experiential knowledge and economic and social needs into their decisions and policies. When among the watermen, I urged watermen and others in the waterman's community to recognize, respect, and incorporate scientific knowledge of the environmental professionals into their planning and decision making efforts for the island and fishery.

I was also, at times, a *sustainer*, finding the resources enabling the weaker party—the Tangiermen—to sustain their challenge. Last, I was an *advocate*, one who not only legitimizes and sustains the challenge of the weaker party but also speaks openly with and for the weaker party, helping those in the weaker roles to identify resources and articulate needs. I advocated and worked to legitimate the involvement of Tangier women and disenfranchised Tangier watermen in the fishery regulatory discussion and decision making.

Paradoxically, the road to peace sometimes runs through increased conflict.[7] This was the case on Tangier. As the researcher, I questioned the status quo, particularly when the status quo excluded people from fully participating in the political process or was anti-biblical, such as promoting illegal acts. Some watermen had a lot to lose if other watermen started obeying fishery laws as the stewardship initiative encouraged. Other people were misinformed or uninformed about the stewardship initiative and were fearful that it would destroy their livelihoods.

As a result, opposition to the effort took the form of death threats against me over the CB radio and ostracization by certain community members, law enforcement harassment of the Tangier watermen who took the stewardship covenant, and name-calling and ostracization of the leaders and members of the FAITH and TaSC groups by family and friends in their own community. In addition, certain people passed around a "dossier" full of falsehoods about one of the outside speakers for the 2020 Vision conference that created fear throughout the community and led to a type of "witch trial" at one of the churches in which I was questioned for two hours.

It was very difficult at times for everyone involved in the stewardship effort and made it imperative, at all times, that the researcher and the stewardship leaders educate people about their motivation for being involved in the effort and remain humble, honest, sincere, loving, and above reproach. Despite the harassment, the watermen and women of the stewardship effort transformed themselves, their community and, unbeknown to them, people around the Chesapeake Bay.

ANALYSIS

For three decades before the stewardship effort, various environmental groups and individuals had promoted an environmental stewardship message on the island. However, they made little headway in affecting the Tangiermen's worldview and behavior. Why did this effort enable such immediate and dramatic changes among the Tangiermen? Charles Kraft, a former anthropologist at Fuller Theological Seminary, developed thirteen factors that influence people's acceptance or rejection of a worldview change. A number of those factors apply to the Tangier case. The reception of the faith and community-based stewardship approach by the Mayor and other Tangier islanders was aided by the following: (1) similarity of the researcher's worldview and language to the community's worldview; (2) economic, technological, and social changes and events that provided a receptive climate to new ideas; (3) recognition that their current perspective was not sufficient to meet the community's felt need; (4) legitimacy of the researcher as a messenger; and (5) recognition that the approach provided a framework to address the community's felt need to maintain their way of life and flowed from their faith-based worldview.[8]

Cultural change took place only when the Tangier people understood that they could generate a solution to their felt need—to maintain their way of life on the island—in a way that would be pleasing to God and according to biblical principles. Thus, Kraft's "fit of idea" and "relation of idea to felt need" were the most important factors in successfully creating transformational change among the people.[9] Using Kraft's terminology, a "cultural peak experience," occurred among Christian and non-Christian islanders upon hearing an environmental stewardship sermon by the researcher during a service that combined both churches on the island. In the pulpit message, using rhetorical questions, the hymn "Jesus Savior Pilot Me," and its iconic imagery, I asked the following:

Is it not inconsistent to call upon Jesus to pilot you and then do to your neighbor and to Creation as you will? Can you be praying, "Thy will be done on earth as it is in heaven" while dumping bait boxes, tin cans and other oil bottles overboard which pollutes God's Creation, or keeping small crabs which takes away the livelihood of your neighbor, and your sons and daughters? In essence, we should place a blindfold over Jesus' eyes [showed "Jesus Pilot Me" picture with blindfold over Jesus' eyes]. What this says is, Yes, Jesus, you can pilot my life through the rough waters of the Bay, but do not watch what I am doing the other ninety-nine percent of the time. . . .[10]

The biblical messages within the sermon and the use of imagery and hymns prompted people to reflect about ways their actions toward the Creation aligned or did not align with the biblical stewardship ethic. One Tangier woman put it this way: "We knew we shouldn't be littering but you helped us see it as something biblical . . . I'm going to pick up my yard today . . . and then help with the neighborhood clean-up."[11] This new understanding led fifty-eight men to kneel at the altar and publicly commit to the "Watermen's Stewardship Covenant." Waterman Jan Marshall's statement reflects the personal transformation that took place among many of the stewardship covenanters in 1998. "I never saw any harm of throwing trash overboard until it was revealed to me that I was damaging my witness for Christ."[12]

As a result of taking the Covenant, many watermen began bringing trash from their boats to the docks, obeying crabbing laws such as not starting work earlier than the law allowed, not taking pregnant crabs, and not placing bait in their peeler pots. A waterman's wife said this, "For the past ten years my husband still will not peeler crab so that he won't be tempted to place bait in his peeler pot."[13]

In a "Women's Stewardship Commitment," a handful of women additionally promised to reuse and recycle materials, change consumption patterns, and teach stewardship and contentment virtues to their children. While the Stewardship Initiative's message did not seem to take hold among all islanders, particularly those who did not take the covenants, ten years later the personal transformation of the lives of both the watermen and women covenanters toward environmental stewardship still remain strong. One of the FAIITH leaders said, "I think that it [stewardship ethic] will always continue because it was a commitment to God. Even my husband, not a person of faith, still brings his bag of trash in from his boat and gets upset when watermen dump things overboard. All of us [covenanters] still share the stewardship message to island visitors at our crab shanties and elsewhere and we still conduct island clean-ups."[14] Another woman covenanter confirmed this truth, "People who were involved from the beginning still try to do their part, but it's the same little group with a few outsiders who try to keep things going."[15]

A linguistic and cultural transformation occurred through the pulpit messages and other stewardship forums that helped the islanders' to discover these convictions: (1) God is both Creator and Redeemer of all his Creation; (2) the Bible requires them to be good stewards of Creation and economies and to obey the civil laws; and (3) stewardship of Creation is part of fulfilling the great commandment—to love the Lord God with all your heart, soul, mind, and strength and to love your neighbor as yourself.

They learned that the Bible teaches that *neighbor* is an inclusive term applied to everyone whom they affect and all those who affect them. A Tangier woman said this: "I realized that my neighbor is everybody who has something to do with the water or can do something to the water like farmers with their runoff."[16] Their "neighbor" now encompassed people who existed beyond their island community, including environmentalists. This led individual Tangiermen to ask forgiveness from CBF staff for ostracizing them and led to CBF staff asking forgiveness for their mistakes.

When asked whether the initiative left any long lasting effects on the relationship between CBF and The Tangier islanders, the vice-president of CBF replied, "We have much stronger support from most of the islanders, with some seemingly life long supporters. Those that were involved in the early initiative continue to support CBF. The decisive nature of the islanders that led to dissent when the initiative was introduced left a small vocal element that we still deal with. The fault was certainly not the initiative, but CBF's ardent fishery policies. However, the initiative became their opportunity to air their dissent."[17]A watermen's wife said this about the current relationship between CBF and the islanders, "We don't see CBF as a threat to us anymore."[18] Yet, another waterman's wife said, "CBF is still not trusted."[19] CBF also had lasting institutional transformation. According to CBF's vice president, "As a result of the initiative, we now have more strong Christians on our island staff.[20] This inevitably influences the way CBF operates, at least on the island.

Hope based on faith in God inspired the Tangier residents to become more politically active. Their activism resulted in the creation of community stewardship meetings and a subsequent 2020 Stewardship Vision plan, a conference for outsiders at which they presented their vision, and the two grassroots organizations—Families Actively Involved in Improving Tangier's Heritage (FAIITH) as well as the Tangier Watermen's Stewardship for the Chesapeake (TaSC), a 501(c)(3) organization. These processes, organizations, and plans empowered the Tangier people by supporting an internal locus of control over their community's environmental, economic, and social affairs.

One year after the initiative, members of TaSC conducted stewardship outreaches to churches in Maryland and Pennsylvania farm communities. Farmers committed to a Farmer Stewardship Covenant and a list of land and water stewardship activities to ensure they would not harm their Tangier "neighbors" down the Bay. Moreover, several TaSC members attempted to implement economic diversification projects, such as oyster pilot projects and a women's data processing co-op, but neither succeeded. The Initiative and its small band of believers could not stop the external economic forces that were rapidly changing the crabbing industry (fuel prices, foreign crab imports, and restrictions of crab permits). Several Tangiermen, including one covenanter, have left crabbing for more financially secure tug boat jobs.

Although FAIITH and TaSC disbanded five years ago, they left an enduring stewardship mindset among the covenanters who will transfer their understanding to the next generation. One of the waterman covenanters said this. "More kids are now conscious of littering and environmental things because of it."[21] Speaking in general about the initiative, the vice-president of CBF said, "The Tangier faith-based stewardship effort left a strong sense of legacy and culture. The Tangier Islanders better appreciate and celebrate their waterman heritage. They are proud to be watermen."[22] Gaining a sense of control over their future by participating in the Initiative also empowered some women to understand better their personal, educational, and entrepreneurial opportunities. Several women involved in the Initiative created a seafood restaurant, still operating, and two others went back to earn college and professional degrees to continue to work and live on the island.

Recognition that their worldview clashed with their biblically based worldview led some islanders to re-evaluate, reinterpret, and repent of their actions. For some Tangier citizens, allegiance to God became paramount and pervaded many more areas of their lives. Their faith-based worldview became more holistic as they applied biblical principles of stewardship, civic virtue, hope, contentment, and forgiveness to their relationships with God, neighbor and Creation.

CONCLUSION

The success of the faith-based and interpersonal approach is evident in the long term personal transformation of attitudes of the covenanters toward responsibility for the island and Bay environment as well as their economy. It also led to increased compliance with civil laws, increased political participation, and better relationships with environmentalists.

The key to the success of this initiative on and beyond Tangier lies in the goals, methodologies, and approaches of the research design. The interpersonal model of engagement provided a framework for a genuine relationship and partnership between the researcher and the Tangier Island citizens to help the Tangiermen in developing their own unique community stewardship initiative based on their faith worldview and their felt need to maintain their waterman-based way of life. Due to the initiative's holistic approach, environmental issues were considered within the context of Tangier's faith-based worldview and its accompanying stewardship ethic, which included means for addressing economic and cultural struggles and conflicts with other stakeholders in the Bay's fisheries. The faith-based and shared-praxis educational approach, aided by the researcher's paracletic role, enabled the Tangiermen to evaluate their attitudes and bring their actions toward the environment, environmentalists, and their local economy into better accord with their faith beliefs. The initiative succeeded because the idea fit their worldview and met their felt need, because the islanders looked at the outside researcher as a messenger with insights that could bring benefits to the community, and because of the inside or island innovators or leaders who included respected men, women, and church and lay leaders.

Researchers can cross-culturally apply faith-based steward-ship with its action-reflection and a shared praxis approach to education to other Christian-based and resource-dependent communities, whether in farming, timber, or ranching localities. Additionally, future researchers could, perhaps, apply it to non-Christian faith-based communities under certain circumstances. In the latter case, they could conduct research using principles from another faith to attempt to achieve the same results. Based on this case, any approach designed to foster change in another community's faith worldview for the benefit of their environ-ment, economy, and relations with environmentalists would need to take into account at least three components: (1) the cul-ture's worldview, faith commitments, and ethical principles re-lated to environmental and economic stewardship and neigh-borliness; (2) the institutional authorities of the culture's faith; and (3) the standards of authority for the culture's faith. In addi-tion, an outside researcher undertaking faith-based stewardship should share all or most of the core convictions of the commu-nity's faith worldview. Finally, action research and a shared-praxis approach to education provide an excellent framework and process for empowering faith-based communities to insti-tute change.

The Tangier Island case study uniquely addresses solutions to changing hearts and minds in the long term toward better stewardship of an island and its blue crab fishery and managing the conflict between a group of resource-dependent people and environmentalists. It does this by generating knowledge with and for the Tangier people and within the context of their com-munity's faith-based worldview, biblical stewardship ethic, and cultural and economic needs.

I based this case study on a liberating understanding of the nature of inquiry—an inquiry that fosters communal movement: movement from the way things are to the way things could be. I set out to foster both personal and social transformation through relationship building. At the heart of the transformations was a research process that involved investigating the circumstances of place and culture; reflecting on the needs, resources, and constraints of the present reality; examining the possible paths; and consciously moving in new directions. Knowledge was generated through a knowing with the mind and heart that incorporated personal and social understandings and authenticated personal and community experiences that led to transformational change.

This case comes at a time when policy and legal arrangements are insufficient in motivating people to care for their environment. We must work within the worldview of people in local communities to truly institute transformational change that makes the bridge between heaven and earth. It has been reported that the missionary James Hudson Taylor recognized people's capabilities to do great things by saying, "How many people estimate difficulties in light of their own resources, and thus attempt little and often fail in the little they attempt. All of God's giants have been weak persons, who did great things for God because they reckoned on him being with them."

NOTES

1. S. E. Smith, D. G. Willms, N. A. Johnson, *Nurtured by Knowledge: Learning to do Participatory Action Research* (New York: The Apex Press, 1997), 5. Smith et.al. quote P. Ekins from his book, *A New World Order: Grassroots Movements for Global Change* (New York: Routledge, Chapman and Hall, 1992), p. 203.

2. "Waterman" is an Old English term referring to people who harvested in more than one fishery—crab, oyster, and fish.

3. Susan Drake Emmerich, *Faith-Based Stewardship and Resolution of Environmental Conflict: An Ethnography of an Action Research Case of Tangier Island Watermen in The Chesapeake Bay* (Ph.D. diss., University of Wisconsin-Madison, 2003), p. 25.

4. Sophie Kerr, "Maryland's Eastern Shore," in *Sound of Petticoats and Other Stories of the Eastern Shore* (New York: Rinehart and Company, 1948 quoted in Wennersten 1992), p. 274.

5. S. E. Smith, p. 181.

6. Y. S. Lincoln and E. G. Guba, *Paradigmatic Controversies, Contradic-*

tions and Emerging Confluences, in *Handbook of Qualitative Research,* 2nd. ed., ed. N. K. Denzin and Y. S. Lincoln (Thousand Oaks: Sage Publications, Inc., 2000), pp. 163-187.

7. R. S. Kraybill, *Repairing the Breach: Ministering in Community Conflict* (Akron, Pa.: Mennonite Central Committee, 1981). In S. D. Emmerich, *Faith-Based Stewardship and Resolution of Environmental Conflict: An Ethnography of an Action Research Case of Tangier Island Watermen in The Chesapeake Bay* (Ph.D. diss., University of Wisconsin-Madison, 2003), p. 38.

8. Charles Kraft, *Christianity in Culture: A Study in Dynamic Biblical Theologizing in Cross-Cultural Perspective* (Marynoll, N.Y.: Orbis Books, 1979), 366-370.

9. Ibid., pp. 366-377.

10. Emmerich, p. 135.

11. Emmerich, p. 177.

12. Ibid., p. 177.

13. Phone interview with Tangier Islander, December 2007.

14. E-mail interview with V.P. of CBF, January 22, 2008

15. E-mail interview with Tangier Islander, January 23, 2008.

16. Emmerich, p. 176.

17. E-mail interview with V.P. of CBF, January 22, 2008.

18. Phone interview with Tangier Islander, December 2007.

19. E-mail interview with Tangier Islander, January 23, 2008.

20. E-mail interview with V.P. of CBF, January 22, 2008.

21. Phone interview with Tangier waterman, January 24, 2008.

22. E-mail interview with V.P. of CBF, January 22, 2008.

Chapter 5

Roundtable Conversation: Hospitality in the Academy

David Thom

David Thom is president of The Leadership Connection, a religious non-profit that he founded in 2003, which he also represents in ministry to faculty at both Harvard University and the Massachusetts Institute of Technology.

Graduating cum laude from the University of Buffalo with a bachelor's degree in philosophy, Thom was employed by Raytheon for two years in Boston before leaving the South Shore to begin his campus ministry career as a Campus Crusade for Christ campus ministry staff member who also represented Athletes in Action at the University of Pennsylvania. After five years, Thom moved from Philadelphia back to Boston for seven years of campus ministry on the Charles River at MIT before moving to the hilly western half of the state for twelve years of ministry at the University of Massachusetts in Amherst.

While in sports ministry with Athletes in Action at UMass, Thom began a ministry focused on coaches and professors under the auspices of Christian Leadership Ministries, the faculty ministry of Campus Crusade. In that process he refined a technique for providing faculty with dinner and discussion events designed to explore the intersection of current academic thought and Christian thought known since 2002 among the five colleges in the Amherst area as The Roundtable on God and Science. In 2005, Thom began The Roundtable on Science, Art & Religion in Cambridge for the purpose of serving faculty at MIT and Harvard. He has since moved his residence closer to Boston—though he still finds himself a long way from the beach.

Faculty at secular colleges and universities typically view their institutions as places where free inquiry reigns. In contrast, many of these faculty view Christian campus ministry organizations on their campuses as bastions for indoctrination. There is some truth to these perceptions. But, a recent phenomenon at some prestigious research universities calls such blanket judgments into question.

In New England's two most secular enclaves, Cambridge and Amherst (Mass.), faculty seminar dinner discussions known since 2002 as The Roundtable have seated hundreds of faculty to explore the intersection of current academic thought and Christian thought. With secular faculty outnumbering their Christian colleagues two to one, college and university scholars regularly assemble, fifty or sixty at a time, for the evening in places like the MIT Faculty Club, the Harvard Faculty Club, or at the Ark Episcopal Chaplaincy Center at UMass-Amherst. Campus ministry professionals know these numbers are remarkable because never in modern campus ministry history have so many secular scholars been assembled so often for discussions which include consideration of Christian thought. In bringing together Christian and secular scholars in unprecedented numbers for face-to-face discussion, in a shift from monologue to dialogue, the Roundtable may be the best means for fostering greater understanding between Christian and secular scholars today.

MESSAGE AS MONOLOGUE

Campus ministry organizations, such as Campus Crusade for Christ and InterVarsity Christian Fellowship (IVCF), have sought to minister to both students and faculty at numerous secular institutions of higher education. Generally viewing such secular institutions as inhospitable to Christian perspectives on knowledge in the academic disciplines and not open to consideration of any knowledge claims informed by a religious source, these campus ministries have sought to cultivate the message of the Christian faith (the good news of the gospel of Jesus Christ) in the lives of Christian students and Christian faculty members. They have aimed to share that message with those on campus who do not profess commitment to the Christian faith. These ministries have also helped Christian faculty members explore ways their faith may inform their teaching and scholarly work.

Such ministries have produced many positive results but have two limitations. First, persons in our college and university communities (or other communities of which we are members) who do not share our Christian faith commitment will not typically flock to the lectures on the Christian message that we sponsor. They rarely hustle to bookstores or libraries to devour the books we Christians write. We then too easily console ourselves with the mistaken notion that when Christian thought has been made available in the written word or through open-invitation lectures our work as Christians is done. Then we convince ourselves that it's not our fault if unbelievers in our communities do not read what we write or listen to what we want to say.

Second, however, is a more significant problem. Those who do not share Christian faith yet who actually read or listen to what Christians write or say often are put off by what turns out to be monologue. To be sure, there may be a modest Q&A session after a public lecture. But posing questions to Christians about their views on given topics is not the same as giving equal time to the articulation of alternative views. In brief, we Christians are all too quick to talk, presenting our understandings of a Christian perspective on the issue at hand, and all too slow to allow those who disagree with us to also have a voice (in a genuine dialogue). We are not sufficiently open to the possibility that a better human, finite glimpse of the "truth" about the issue at hand may actually emerge from such genuine dialogue.

One can understand this focus on monologue. After all, if you believe you have the truth, what is there to discuss? Discussion will only muddy the waters; the results may be inconclusive. It may be hard to point to immediacy of results. And, if anything seems paramount in the thinking of many Christians, especially those of an evangelical bent, it is the need for immediate, conclusive results, preferably quantifiable (such as the number of conversions to the Christian faith or the number of attendees at a lecture given by a prominent Christian spokesperson). This expectation is exacerbated by the fact that those who provide financial support for campus ministries are too often enamored of reports of such quantifiable "success."

It takes courage to forsake donor-driven lecture models if they're not actually attracting secular consideration. We need to encourage experimentation until we find methods that actually work. To give up what donors like to spend money on means possibly losing their support. And while searching for new methods that actually attracts secular individuals to consider Christian thought, we may first try experiments that fail.

The highlight of the Roundtable programs in Amherst and Cambridge is rejection of the monologue approach to proclaiming a message. Rather, a Christian message is embedded within a genuine dialogue with scholars not committed to Christian faith.

THE ROUNDTABLE

The two Roundtables currently offered are *The Five-College Roundtable on God and Science* (the five colleges are UMass-Amherst, Smith, Mount Holyoke, Amherst, and Hampshire), and *The Cambridge Roundtable on Science, Art & Religion* (focusing on faculty at Harvard and MIT). A listing of all Roundtable events offered at these two sites since 2002 (twenty-one in Amherst and ten in Cambridge through autumn 2009), with name and affiliations of presenters, is at www.amherstroundtable.org and www.cambridgeroundtable.org.

Presenters have included such notable scholars as Owen Gingerich (Harvard), Jean Bethke Elshtain (Chicago), John Polkinghorne (Cambridge), George Marsden (Notre Dame), and Harry Lewis (former dean, Harvard College). Each of these Roundtables is chaired by highly respected members of the faculty or administration at a participating college or university.

Each Roundtable event focuses on a pre-announced topic at the "intersection of current academic thought and Christian thought." One or two prominent scholars are invited to be presenters at the Roundtable (albeit not in the usual sense of being a "presenter"). If there is one presenter, he or she is not necessarily a Christian, since the main role of the presenter is to inspire good discussion. If there are two presenters (which occurs for about half of the Roundtables), then one will be a Christian.

Each event is by invitation only, to keep the total number of participants near fifty and to enable the proceedings to focus on dialogue between participants. Given the topic for discussion, faculty and academic deans with departmental affiliations judged to have interest are invited, and all prior participants are invited back as well. About ten percent of the participants are clergy or campus ministry chaplains along with a financial sponsor or two. Invitations are distributed by e-mail, requesting an RSVP. The invitation makes it clear that "The Roundtable does not sponsor presenters to endorse or promote any particular point of view." Participants who accept invitations are directed to the Roundtable websites where presenters have made readings available to prepare all participants for the Roundtable event.

Each Roundtable begins with about thirty minutes of hors d'oeuvres, including beer and wine, served immediately upon arrival. Participants then find their assigned seats around tables, with from six-eight persons per table. Participants are assigned to each table to insure a diverse group that will lend itself to a stimulating conversation.

After all participants are seated, as moderator I introduce the presenter(s) and describe the evening's proceedings. A single presenter will then take about fifteen minutes for opening comments that summarize the highlights of his or her readings. (If there are two presenters, each will take about fifteen minutes.)

A catered dinner is now served. During dinner, the participants at each table discuss the topic at hand for about an hour. Then as moderator I lead the whole group in discussion in a plenary session for about another hour, and, if necessary, I gently guide the session away form Q&A with the presenters and focus the discussion between the participants. The Roundtable participants are then dismissed after this group discussion.

Total cost for a Roundtable is usually $3,000-6,000. Funds are provided by individual donors or a foundation that has offered to pick up costs when individual donors fail to do so.

We have found that the dialogues started at the Roundtable events have continued in some ad hoc settings, over breakfast, lunch, and coffee. The evidence is that many participants at Roundtable events are glad to be able to continue sharing their beliefs and experiences relative to a recent Roundtable topic long after the Roundtable event.

To say that these Roundtable events have been well received by participating scholars holding to differing religious commitments, or who consider themselves non-religious, is a gross understatement. What is it that has made these Roundtable events attractive to this wide spectrum of scholars at these prestigious colleges and universities? We can identify four reasons that contribute to scholars wanting to attend a Roundtable.

- The Roundtable chairs are highly respected members of the local college or university communities.
- The featured presenters have excellent academic credentials and scholarly accomplishments that a wide spectrum of scholars find compelling.
- Faculty enjoy the opportunity to socialize with their peers in intercollegiate and interdisciplinary settings, especially in an environment of welcoming hospitality.
- The evening is academic in nature but is nevertheless a rare opportunity to talk about ultimate truths, virtues, values, and meaning in life as well as to share one's beliefs and experiences relative to these crucial issues.

But what kind of experiences do Roundtable participants have? By e-mail, participants are asked to evaluate their Roundtable experience. If one looks for patterns in these comments, the following two major reasons emerge for why participants have found these Roundtables to be eminently worthwhile. (An exhaustive list of evaluative comments from participants can be accessed at the two web sites noted above.)

Participants have found that the Roundtable events have exemplified respectful conversations about differing points of view relative to the announced topic, without favoring any one point of view.

Since this evaluation is central to the purpose of the Roundtable, pertinent evaluative quotes are presented below:

> We [at our table] engaged in a lively discussion of the topic
> at hand despite some wildly differing backgrounds. It was

interesting to talk to people whose ideas I had never encountered before, and whose perspective I could not necessarily guess right away.

Our table discussion and the plenary discussion were both enlightening and did a lot in my mind to tear down some of the stereotypes that each group [Christians, Muslims, and unaffiliated] had about the other. At the same time, we could talk about our differences as well as learn how we can talk about our differences.

Dinner is always a good idea! The discussion was very engaging and fruitful. I was able to hear my own thoughts on the topic being articulated by others in novel ways. I also was forced to consider perspectives that did not come naturally to me. [This evaluative comment reminds one of the claim that the sign having really listened to another is being able to state her position to her satisfaction.]

Participants appreciated the opportunity to talk about important interdisciplinary issues that were broader than the more specialized issues within their respective academic disciplines. Witness, for example, the following evaluative comment:

The best part of this whole series, and especially last evening, is that it forces me to stop and think about some of the broader issues that I otherwise don't find time to do, being lost in the minutia of research and teaching. What should we be teaching is certainly a question all professors should ask themselves. It got me thinking whether I should be teaching something broader than the narrow technical astrophysics courses aimed at our majors and grad students, and whether we should be giving our majors and grad students a broader view of astronomy and physical science in general. I think the answer to both is yes.

Our Roundtable participants also felt free to offer critical evaluative comments and suggestions for improving subsequent Roundtable events. First, there was a recurring concern over the gender imbalance among participants. Where were the women scholars? In fact, as many female as male scholars were invited, but many could not come because of after-hours family commitments.

A second pattern of concerns was a sense that the conversations, both around the tables and especially in the closing plenary discussion, could have been more focused. A constructive suggestion for future Roundtables was to prepare a list of questions each table would discuss, with focus on these questions then carrying over to the closing plenary session along with more guidance for discussion provided by the moderator.

There was mixed opinion regarding the limited amount of time given to the featured presenters. Most participants seemed to appreciate the fact that lengthy lectures were not given, allowing much time for conversation. But, some felt that it was a shame that so little time was given to hearing from such world-renowned scholars. In a few cases, this problem was solved when featured presenters agreed to give lectures or participate in debates a day before or after a Roundtable event.

A concern was also expressed that some participants tended to "hog the conversation." What else is new? The suggestion was made that the moderator tell the gathered group at the outset of the Roundtable that "each participant should talk only once until everyone has had a chance to talk."

One suggestion for refining the program for future Roundtables was that the scope of participants be expanded to include a few extraordinarily prominent community leaders to engage with scholars on topics that can benefit from the insights of both scholars and community leaders. It has been our experience that most scholars simply prefer to be in the company of other scholars, because otherwise the dialogue might have a tendency toward being watered-down or distorted. However, a prominent community leader has participated, and others have shown an interest. Thus if the number of community participants is kept to just a few per Roundtable, Roundtables may indeed come to be known as a safe place for community leaders to network among a plurality of scholars.

Our most recent Roundtables were our highest in attendance (in the sixties) and featured Rice University sociologist Michael Lindsay sharing from his book, *Faith in the Halls of Power*,[1] where he discusses the impact those of Christian evangelical faith are already having in the more influential areas of U.S. culture. At this time of editing we are looking forward to Yale University Law Professor Amy Chua visiting with us to discuss her recent book, *Day of Empire*,[2] where she argues that racial and religious tolerance on the part of superpower nations enhances their prospects for perpetuity and prosperity and that such prosperity also awaits the superpower universities that grant Christians the unequivocal freedom to identify publicly as Christians in their scholarship and teaching.

In summary, Christian faculty members in Amherst and Cambridge and a few select chaplains have recognized that if the modern secular university is ever going to reverse course and promote the discussion of Christian thought, then we are going to need to demonstrate that the discussion of Christian thought actually enhances free inquiry and brings about the potential for added depth to the work of faculty as scholars and educators. This is the very commitment we have made with the Roundtable format, and our continued faithfulness to achieving this objective is why individual scholars continue to return.

HOSPITALITY

Christians are encouraged to "extend hospitality" (Rom. 12:13), to "be hospitable to one another" (1 Pet. 4:9). A dictionary definition of *hospitality* includes "given to generous and cordial reception of guests" or "offering a pleasant or sustaining environment." Beyond a cordial reception of guests, however, the hospitality we offer at Roundtables has two more dimensions.

First, we provide an environment in which participants feel free to share their own beliefs and supporting experiences relative to the topic under discussion, possibly leading to common ground. In addition, when such common ground is not attainable, we provide our guests with a welcoming space within which to disagree with one another. To illustrate this latter dimension of hospitality, consider the following observation of one of the participants at a Roundtable that featured Rev. Dr. John Polkinghorne as the presenter:

> The speaker [Polkinghorne] . . . has a wonderful hospitality.
> By that I mean something far beyond politeness or graciousness. Rather, in his arguing for his own views and explanation as to why he does not hold certain alternative views he never puts anyone else down. Quite the reverse:

he creates safe space for real encounter between people of differing views.

In a nutshell, then, *the hospitality we offer is to graciously welcome our participants as special guests, to give each one the freedom to express a point of view and the reasons and experiences supporting that point of view, and to provide a welcoming space to express disagreements with other participants.* With that commitment, our intent for our Roundtables is to offer the gift of hospitality not only to those who do not share our Christian faith but to all the faculty: Our Roundtable hospitality is meant as a gift to the university. To dig beneath the surface, there are two byproducts of such hospitality that lay the foundation for persons in conversation being open to listening respectfully to those who do not share their beliefs: empathetic relationships and trust.

Most people would agree that it is easier to talk about disagreements with those you have gotten to know well enough to understand why they believe and live as they do. Genuine dialogue can emerge from such empathetic relationships.

Establishing such an empathetic relationship also breeds trust. It is all too easy for Christians to demonize persons we do not know who do not share our faith and for those not committed to Christian faith to demonize Christians not known on a personal level. Such distrust is rampant in the academy and elsewhere in contemporary culture. But when we extend the gift of hospitality to another, we have taken a giant step toward breaking down those barriers of distrust, opening up the possibility of genuine dialogue. Such interpersonal dynamics have been at play, we believe, in our Roundtables, leading to genuine dialogue between people who disagree with one another about important and often controversial issues.

When guest speakers proclaim a message to a crowd from a distance of ninety feet or authors proclaim a message to readers from a distance akin to 900 miles, their illustrations and personal stories, winsomeness, and non-combative vocabulary may go a long way toward making up that distance, but it cannot go where face-to-face interaction can go. *The length of distance exponentially voids the potential for understanding.* Face-to-face exchange is packed with the potential for understanding. We have observed that in a hospitality-guided setting, where the gift of sustenance and the pleasure of eating hovers in celebration over the assembly, listening in thankfulness is easier. Therefore being understood is much more naturally possible, and that is what people want: to be heard and understood. As important as truth is, it may never be received or understood as well as it could be if it is not pursued in an environment of hospitality. Consider the following reflections from Leon Kass:

> Far from being an escape from the serious demands of life, witty and convivial dining—a species of high play—pays tribute to the meaningfulness of human life and its possibilities for community, freedom, and nobility—all in the act of sustaining life through nourishment. Further, the detachment needed for wit and laughter is akin to that needed for seeking truth, and the free play of the mind in conversation often provides food for deeper thought. Philosophy, it used to be said, begins in wonder, and there is much that is wonder-ful in the things seen and heard around the dinner table. Dining is both excellent in itself and a token of something more: Its amiability anticipates friendship, its free speech anticipates pursuit of truth or philosophy, its beauty (or nobility) promises and beckons to the good.[3]

Hospitality has within it accepted rules of conduct that dramatically enhance the opportunity for a special kind of beauty between participants who are handling delicate subject matter. There is a shared feeling among participants at Roundtable events that something unique and fruitful is being achieved: A mutual sense of understanding is taking place over an extended period as participants return to dinners several times over. Participants often remark how they enjoy the intense and insightful discussion. New participants often comment how surprised they are to have been able to enter difficult discussions so freely and openly. We celebrated achieving such continued openness, respect, and teachability among scholars who have clearly different positions on Christian thought.

I close this section on hospitality with a note on the progression I experienced in my twenty years of student ministry. In working with athletes at the University of Pennsylvania and the University of Massachusetts—Amherst, with Chinese athletes during four summers of ministry in China, and with fraternity brothers (who were also athletes) at MIT, my strategy was to extend the gift of hospitality, thereby first building relationships of mutual trust, before sharing with them my understanding of the Christian faith. Since a hospitable approach worked in ministering to students, I wasn't surprised that hospitality would be valued by faculty.

But, I did not invent the idea of hospitality. The biblical record contains potent examples of the practice of hospitality in the ministry of Jesus and in the early Christian church.

HOSPITALITY IN THE BIBLICAL RECORD

Consider the extraordinary extent to which Jesus had face-to-face contact with people. He delighted in being with people in ways that a lecturer cannot. He was a frequent guest at dinners and parties. He spent inordinate amounts of time with the outcasts and marginalized of his society, including tax collectors and prostitutes. And that included eating and drinking with those rejected by the religious people of his day to an extent that caused some to label him a drunkard. He had an urgent message to give to those he engaged, but his message was generally delivered in a context of unhurried hospitality.

Consider his engagement at a well with a woman of Samaria (John 4: 1-30): The woman came to draw water, and Jesus, being thirsty, asked her for a drink (a simple act of hospitality). What ensued was a fascinating conversation, during which the woman felt free to share the details of a life that was not well lived, and Jesus responded with a message of hope. But, the disciples of Jesus didn't get it, for they could only marvel that "he was speaking with a woman" (4: 27). Jesus had created an hospitable space where he and the woman could talk openly about the path the woman's life had taken, and, in the case of Jesus, the path he would walk in days to come. The conversation changed the women's life. And consider how Jesus describes the beginning of a relationship with him in metaphorical terms of *hospitality*: "Listen, I am standing at the door, knocking; if you hear my voice and open the door, I will come into you and eat with you, and you with me" (Rev. 3:20).

The book of the Acts of the apostles is replete with examples of offering the gift of hospitality. Robert Coleman has pointed out that only one quarter of the verses in Acts are devoted to sermons or proclamation and that only one third of the words used in verbal communication in Acts indicate formal delivery[4]. Ordinary social interaction is the primary context for the ministry of the early Christian church, and instances of hospitality often set the stage for that ministry. Consider some examples, first of providing opportunity to share experiences, and then providing the opportunity to express disagreements.

The disciples often ministered through shared experiences. Acts 2 begins with the disciples "speaking of the mighty deeds of God" and Peter addressing those gathered in Jerusalem to observe Pentecost, a religious feast of generous hospitality shared among strangers. Addressing his audience, Peter identifies not privileged kings, princes, and priests, but common folk sharing common experiences: "sons and daughters . . . young men . . . old men . . . slaves, both men and women. . . . " Peter reminds them of the nature of their shared experience: "You that are Israelites, listen to what I have to say: Jesus of Nazareth, *a man attested to you by God with deeds of power, wonders, and signs that God did through him among you, as you yourselves know. . .* " (2:22, emph. added). As the chapter concludes, we are given, in a cherished passage of Scripture, a bird's-eye view of the church's emphasis on hospitality: "Day by day, as they spent much time together in the temple, they broke bread at home and ate their food with glad and generous hearts" (2:46).

Valuing hospitality is not an invention of the church; it's the practice of any healthy community. Whereas Jesus and the disciples could proclaim certain truths to their Jewish audience because of their common backgrounds and shared experiences, the polarities of background and experience that exist between modern religious and non-religious communities lead to the monologue of failed proclamation. The failure emerges from the fact that individuals and communities do *not* already share similar experiences. Without the common ground of similar experiences, we need to ask whether persistently practicing the monologue of proclamation in our era might ultimately make reaching shared understandings that much more difficult.

These few examples from Scripture give guidance for the present: Rather than valuing only certain experiences, the early church had respect for the experiences of others, and it shared its own insights while respecting the experience of others, so as to not allow any group or individual to lord it over others. When the monologue of proclamation marks what secular scholars perceive they know best about the church and its scholars, the modern church is perceived as much too guarded about interaction and therefore insecure about its scholarship. In the words of Paul (1 Cor. 9:20), we should strive to share as much understanding as possible with those whom we hope to bless: "To the Jews I became as a Jew, in order to win Jews. To those under the law, I became as one under the law (though I myself am not under the law) so that I might win those under the law." Taking the initiative to begin with hospitality and shared experiences may ultimately mean delaying many routine uses of proclamation because proclamation best rests upon some common ground.

In summary, the text gives us precedent for understanding the gift of hospitality as providing opportunities for conversation about various points of view and the reasons and experiences supporting them. Lectures do not produce the same lasting and memorable interpersonal communication.

Where there is little if any common ground relative to points of view and the supporting reasons and experiences, it is wise to choose hospitality over proclamation to begin the journey toward relationship. This is why the Roundtable limits presenters to fifteen minutes and why the focus of the event is on the contributions of all of the participants—not just the presenter. In contemporary campus ministry proclamation methodology, the subtle impression given to others is that the Goliath-like champion presenter/proclaimer can take on all questions, comments, and complaints. That attitude smacks of intimidation, manipulation, and naked power, which is not the kind of impression that will stir in others the desire for listening and understanding.

In addition to an emphasis on building on shared experiences within the Christian church, the book of Acts also provides compelling examples of first-century Christians providing each other with a welcoming space to express disagreements. As recorded in Acts 10, 11, and 15, a contentious issue in the early church was whether membership in the church should be limited to Jewish believers. Could converted Gentiles also be included? The preliminary answer was a theologically-based non-experiential emphatic "no" with hundreds of years of theological, cultural, and political support for keeping non-Jews on the margins of Jewish communities.

But then the apostles Peter and James were given the opportunity to tell the Jewish Christian community (particularly the Jerusalem Council) about their first-hand experiences with Gentile followers of Jesus and how these experiences testified to the genuineness of the commitment of the Gentiles to the Christian faith. Their persuasive report on their positive experiences with Gentile followers of Jesus led the Jerusalem Council to embrace these new believers within the body of Christ (see Acts 15).

CONCLUSION

Roundtables ask for participants to engage in genuine dialogue, which involves not only the listening of those outside of the church but also the listening *of* the church. Those outside of the church have virtually ceased to attend Christian lectures or read Christian literature. The truth of the matter is that in our day and age of contentiousness in religion and politics, all too few people expect to be listened to. If we give the gift of listening to those who do not share our faith, they may even grant us the gift of listening—and a genuine dialogue can then take place.

If you are willing to first listen, you may even find that the very act of listening can disarm those who come to the table intent on not listening to anything you may want to say. One of the best illustrations of turning a lecture into an opportunity for listening is recounted by Kelly Monroe Kullberg. Intending to deliver a presentation on feminism at a major state university, Kelly found

> More than three hundred angry students, ten Southern Baptists off to the side in mild shock, and me. A chalkboard and chalk. And no security trained in crowd control. . . . "Lord," I asked, sitting with the chanters. "I'm just curious; what are YOU planning on doing tonight? I can barely wait to hear what the speaker has to say." He shared the thought, "We're going to scrap the slide show about women around the world with the pretty music." "Right," I replied. "And then what?" "Go to the chalkboard and start writing down what they're saying. Listen to them. Show them how to listen, how to take turns speaking, that I care about what

they're saying and feeling." "Right, then what?" "I'll tell
you when you need to know." So I went to the chalkboard
and started to write.[5]

Kullberg turned a session planned for one hour into a four-
hour genuine conversation. The conversation was set in motion
by her simply being willing to listen, disarming her militantly
hostile audience through her sincere capacity to listen and understand.

Do you want others to hear a message you think they need to
hear? Start by listening. Why should they listen to you, if you
will not take the first step of listening to them? Create an hospitable environment in which others will feel like guests, and
they will often respond as a valued guest responds. We desper-
ately need such hospitality in the academy. And Christians
should be quick to extend that gift.

Why care what the Roundtable might accomplish over time?
Christians have often been known for careening (swaying or
swerving) and careering (making a career) away from intellectual life, to such an extent that ministries have ventured onto
campus only to save students spiritual lives but not with any respect for the academy itself. Unfortunately, over time, the unin-
tended message communicated that the academy itself and its
leaders can "go to hell" while ministries focus exclusively on
students.

Might it be worth the effort, however, to attempt to affect the
university as a whole? Is higher education truly all that meaningful or influential? Is scholarship all that consequential? Do
the educators themselves really matter? Yes. *Time's* Person of the
Century was Albert Einstein: not a statesman nor a soldier nor an
athlete nor an entertainer nor a member of the clergy—but a
Princeton professor. Arguably the most influential Christian
writer over the last century was professor C. S. Lewis. Though
scholars at heart, both Einstein and Lewis left legacies far beyond their areas of academic expertise. Each, caring about *the big
picture*, was conversant on any number of topics important to
modern people right into our present century.

The intellectual life is something extraordinary, shared in
common only by God and by human beings made in his image.
Jesus is not only Lord of the Bible study and of the pew but of the
library and of the classroom. In the recovery of domain that

properly belongs to the Lord, the God of the universe will not share his glory with another. When reclaiming things that belong to him, restoration will not come about by force or by our frail wisdom or judgment.

> "All these things my hand has made,
>   and so all these things are mine,"
>   says the Lord.
> "But this is the one to whom I will look,
>   to the humble and contrite in spirit
>   who trembles at my word." (Isa. 66:2)

What God has made God also lays claim to, in order to bring a blessing. We are not contending that the universities themselves actually belong to the Lord; brick and mortar are not his domain. Rather, he is Lord of the spaces shared by the Christian in the university, spaces the Christian can redeem by taking the initiative to be a blessing in his or her community. We cannot go to war with the academy in the hope of redeeming its function and purpose. In a humble and contrite spirit, choosing to serve colleagues in the academy by offering the gift of hospitality is the way to begin to be God's blessing to the university.

NOTES

1. Michael Lindsay, *Faith in the Halls of Power* (New York: Oxford University Press, 2007).

2. Amy Chua, *Day of Empire* (New York: Doubleday, 2007).

3. Leon R. Kass, *The Hungry Soul* (Chicago: University of Chicago Press, 1994), p.183.

4. Robert E Coleman, *The Master Plan of Discipleship* (Grand Rapids, Mich.: Revell, 1987), pp. 32, 88.

5. Kelly Monroe Kullberg, *Finding God Beyond Harvard* (Downers Grove, Ill.: InterVarsity Press, 2006), p. 69.

Chapter 6

Changing the Culture, One Film at a Time

Jack Hafer

Jack Hafer is the President of Boulevard Pictures, located in Culver City, California. Hafer is the producer of the award-winning feature film *To End All Wars*, starring Kiefer Sutherland and Robert Carlyle. It won Best Picture at the Heartland Film Festival; was awarded the Commander in Chief Medal of Service, Honor, and Pride by the Veterans of Foreign Wars; and was showcased at the 2003 Cannes Film Festival Cinema for Peace. Hafer has several feature films currently in development.

He produced the PBS documentary *Wall Of Separation*, on the separation of church and state in America, that aired in June/July 2007, and is currently working on four more documentaries.

As former Vice President and General Manager of GMT Studios in Culver City, Hafer oversaw the complete operations of this state-of-the-art film studio, best known for film projects such as *L.A. Story, Wag the Dog, Little Man Tate, Philadelphia Experiment, Predator,* and *Tequila Sunrise.*

I am frequently asked as a person of faith how I can work in the often-secular film industry. So let me mention this at the start: First, I am not angry with Hollywood. I'm part of Hollywood. I am a member of the Producers Guild of America. Part of my identity is here. Certainly, a great deal of my life is here. So I speak from Hollywood.

Thus, when I make movies as a Christian, it's not with an us/them mentality. Yes, I'm a Christian, but these are my friends, even when they're not of the same faith. I respect what they do—we breathe the same air. If I'm disappointed in certain films, it's because I want my friends to succeed, and I don't think some films help a career. I expect more than that from my friends.

I don't live in a secular culture, if that means there are no religions there. I live in a pluralistic culture—a culture full of religions. Roy Clouser's book, *The Myth of Religious Neutrality*[1] is helpful here. There is a legitimate desire in American culture to not have one faith take over and run the rest of us out of town. In that regard, the separation of church and state is a very good thing. We all live with our various faiths and express them in a way that allows society to work.

Does that mean, then, that I don't believe in the proclamation of my faith? No. I allow for proclamation, given certain parameters. But love for the other person and consideration of that person's faith-system must guide any discussion of one's personal faith. As long as I'm being a person and not a salesman, as long as I respect another's dignity, I have the right to discuss my faith in the right context. I am never selling persons something, if selling means ignoring a person. I'm more comfortable with the idea of dialogue—the give-and-take of true conversation about meaningful things, which (see more below) is part of the Great Conversation

The Christian is always a member of two communities, the specifically Christian community (the church), and the larger society in which she lives. As a Christian, the individual must decide how she is going to participate in each community. In the first, there is a shared basis of authority (Scriptures and the tradition) that doesn't exist in the second group. Thus the language in which he expresses himself will be different. And film is involved with the second language.

As a Christian who is involved in the business of making films, I want to create films regarded by my Hollywood peers as well-made and that attain the goals for the film, whether sheer entertainment or something more. The content, tone, and style of the film can build a mutual trust between filmmakers who are mutually involved in the great conversation.

But given this introduction, what am I doing with my films? I am making films for three reasons: to spread truth, to recapture the sacred, and to build cultural cohesion. In doing that, I am required to appreciate the tradition of filmmaking and to carry on the great conversation. I will elaborate, but as I describe these, I want it to be clear that to approach film in this way means I don't make "Christian" films, as some have understood that term; rather, I make films that deal with the human condition and thereby invite people of all persuasions to find themselves in them in some way.

SPREAD TRUTH

My role in making a film, as I see it, is the same as that of any storyteller. And that is to interpret the world from a certain perspective. As a Christian, however, my purpose is to use whatever perspective shapes film to offer truth.

One example of such a truth is the need to recognize the existence and importance of the human soul. Truth is not an agreed-upon concept today, but in my world truth includes the idea that the human soul requires tending to. It can grow if fed or atrophy if ignored. This is not just a materialistic world but has a spiritual aspect as well. This is what great literature was all about—great literature dealt with the great issues of the soul in great ways. The Enlightenment through which we've arrived at our contemporary cultural perspectives did not always appreciate that. It started off with some great goals but got lost in the process. It wanted to use the scientific method to discover more about nature but then asked of science what science was not capable of delivering. Enlightenment thinkers wanted to use the scientific method in areas where it didn't work and thus ended up with an inadequate view of life stressing a materialism that practically denied man's soul and its needs.

Science and the scientific method brought us a great deal of knowledge and continues to do so. In politics, for example, the Enlightenment's insights helped improve an understanding of Christianity's role in the public square. It helped teach Christians that religious freedom, freedom of conscience, is important to defend and helps Christians resist temptation to impose their views on a society. I greatly appreciate such contributions of the Enlightenment. But it left many of us empty when it tried to limit all human experience to rationalism. The ability to reason is one of our most important blessings, but the use of reason to find truth doesn't mean that we can't also discern truth through the mixing of reason with intuition; the experience of art, beauty, the mysterious; or the blessings of revelation.

It seems shallow to me to deny the enchantment of things, things above materialism. Others have felt this as well. I have greatly appreciated Morris Berman's book, *The Reenchantment of the World*[2] and Suzi Gablik's books on the re-enchantment of art.[3] These books are deep calling to deep—they ring a note at home deep within us. Thus the importance of the soul is one truth that I hope for the films to imply.

RECAPTURE THE SACRED

In addition to my desire to spread truth, I desire to use the sacred. I personally have a need for life to be sacred, for life to include sacred ingredients. The sacred has two different but related meanings in this regard. The sacred means religious as opposed to secular (non-religious). That is, it has to do with those things associated with or dedicated to God or regarded with reverence because of such dedication. The second meaning of sacred is that of sacrosanct; here something is reverenced or respected because it's a part of our time-tested tradition and therefore secure from violation or damage. I want life to have those sacred things, things set apart, regarded as special and not violated or treated lightly. I believe that when the sacred is removed, we miss much of what life has to offer.[4]

So I hope for the films I create to make life seem sacred, even spiritual. The spiritual aspect of life is perhaps a step beyond just being sacred. It has to do with that aspect of life that is not just physical but which gives meaning to the soul. The physical story will have a spiritual side to it. The person interested in spiritual formation is interested in developing more depth of personhood and/or a deeper relationship with God. Marx, Freud, and Darwin, our popularizers of Nietzsche, for all their contributions (and their misunderstandings), needed to add another dimension to their thinking. Science by itself just seems to lack a depth. It misses warmth, emotion, passion, things that touch us on a deep level.

The arts should provide those moments of silence, of epiphany and reflection, reminding us of the spiritual side of life. This includes the idea of good over bad. But it also includes the idea of man's humility in the face of the noumena—Rudolph Otto's "other," "holy," "awe" in *The Idea of the Holy*.[5]

This can be done with an amazing number of subjects in film. Consider the number of films that have been dealing with the supernatural and spirituality, such as these: *Dead Man Walking, Agnes of God, Shawshank Redemption, The Big Kahuna, Simon Birch, The Green Mile, Magnolia, Contact, Meet Joe Black, The Sixth Sense, The Others, The End of the Affair, The Third Miracle, The Devil's Advocate, Grand Canyon, L.A. Story, Phenomena, Michael, City of Angels, Signs.*

BUILD CULTURAL COHESION

A third reason to make films is to help build cultural cohesion. When we risk seeing everything as relative, amid so many different religions and perspectives, can we ever find any agreed-upon authority or some form of agreed-upon thinking that will bring real stability to society through its unity?

What is the present authority in our culture? Through all of the scientific age the West lived off the capital of Judeo-Christianity. Our cultural cohesion was inherited, not really chosen. As that cohesion was challenged in the past century, especially the 1920s and the 1960s and after, it has seemed that there is no unity in our society. But now that there is an admission of the failure of the Enlightenment, of a mechanistic answer, the possibility of a new cohesion is before us. What is that cohesion?

I suggest that it could be the sheer admission of the reality of spirituality. Some have referred to this as enchantment (C. S. Lewis being one). Enchantment suggests elves and goblins in children's stories. By enchantment, however, I mean that the parts and parcels of life are endowed with meaning by the overall story. Our meta-narrative interprets the facts and events for us. Things have meaning. Enchantment was for Lewis a door into the life of the imagination. Though the idea of enchantment is far less than the Judeo-Christian or Muslim God, it is still a call for more than the physical. So whether we call it enchantment or refer to it with the more religious term *spiritual*, here is an area being rediscovered in our society as something we had forgotten existed.

Art lost its purpose when we took away the spiritual. It became just self-expression, Tom Wolfe's flatness,[6] sheer art for art's sake. There was no message or meaning. It didn't serve a higher purpose. But we can now ask spiritual questions in our art.

This cohesion from the recognition and acceptance of a spiritual side to life doesn't do away with tolerance, multiculturalism, or pluralism, in their finest definitions. It allows for each person to choose but doesn't denigrate the person who chooses the spiritual answer or path. Hence, religion and the spiritual has recovered a legitimate place in society. The public square is no longer naked.

September 11, 2001, briefly made this clear to us. For a few days, things changed. We all were admittedly spiritual. The atheists could still be atheists if they wanted, even though I could not see their basis of goodness. But they could no longer require that the public square avoid all expressions of faith—the common-sense element had become too obvious. Everyone was praying and talking about prayer—even the anchorpersons on the national news channels.

Sin was real. The word *evil* was actually used. What could deal with such real evil? What could bring solace to so much suffering? Humanity was brought to its knees—we recognized our weakness in light of such a huge problem. Our secure world was turned upside down. We were all at a great funeral, and at a funeral such spiritual thoughts, along with humility and love, are acceptable.

The tribalization of America was, for a while, overcome by the response to 9-11. Unity came from working together on a common goal or being pulled together over a common loss. September 11 has long since passed and the unity with it, but there is a residue remaining. The crack in the wall was made, and the public square is now tolerating, if not hosting, the sacred. It wasn't just 9-11 that did it—other disappointments played into it as well. Yet in this fresh context, the artist is freed to pursue unanswered questions, and the artist's asking of such questions allows us all to ask our own. So that now, more than ever, the artist is no longer just an individualist, a voice crying in the wilderness. The artist is a part of the community of those looking for more.[7]

Appreciate the Tradition

In going after the aforementioned goals in filmmaking, one must remember both the tradition and the great conversation. First, a reminder about tradition. I am inspired by Greg Wolfe of *Image*[8] journal at times like these, and I am indebted to him for some of the following thoughts. He reminds us that we still need individual expression, creativity, and new ways of looking at life, but that individualism lost all meaning when it was set loose from cultural identity and institutional authority. Individualism becomes meaningless when it is removed from the community out of which and against which it spoke. There is nothing to rebel against when there is no there there.

T. S. Eliot is my role model here. He told us that we can't make *avant garde* art when we don't know the Tradition. Whether we like it or not, we are part of a tradition. And as we create art, we enter into the history of that process at a certain time. We must know the vocabulary to communicate. We must know how we fit into the process or our art borders on loss of communication and triviality. And thus we must study the Tradition to get our voice.

How we say what we say in film is then crucial. We must know how the film language works and not try to make a feature film carry more than it can. When we consider topics for films, or stories, we must bring our understanding of where the craft is operating today to our making of the film. For example, cultural cohesion is a legitimate goal of art—but some caveats are in order. This goal must be pursued with wisdom. Unity isn't necessarily always good. There is a time to take a stand for truth amid which the possibility of cohesion may suffer. And the artist must continually be aware of that.

We must also understand that we "see in a mirror, dimly" (1 Cor. 13:12), and all our efforts are tainted with our own perspectives. The peace that Jesus asked us to pray for is destroyed in too many instances by the church itself. Many Christians have contributed to the unwanted divisions in our country, and not in a legitimate way. Religious separatism—the belief in purification by separation—has been a central area of misunderstanding all down through American church history.

The early 1900s Modernist-Fundamentalist debate caused conservatives to withdraw from the public realm. This may strengthen local subcultures but weakens culture at broader levels. What is gained in internal purity is lost in relation to Christians' needed impact on the cultural mainstream.

As we consider where we are today, we tend to fall into one of two positions in relation to the arts. We need to be those who appreciate truth wherever we find it, and yet we tend to be either reactionary or traditional. Reactionaries believe that nothing valid has been produced since the demise of their favorite historical epoch. Traditionalists believes that culture is a living thing, even in times of adversity.[9]

We must care about the art and literature of our day. Many don't. They appreciate the classics without realizing how innovative the classics were in their own day. Reactionaries pay homage to the classics, in part, because they see these works as if they were under glass. As Gregory Wolfe has said, reactionaries live in the past precisely because the past does not live in them.[10]

The Christian filmmaker must attempt to bring a peace and cohesion to society, finding the things that can be affirmed and encouraged, whenever possible. We must take leadership in making goodness look attractive, wherever it is found.

CARRY ON THE GREAT CONVERSATION

When Will Hutchens and Mortimer Adler published their *Great Books of the Western World* in 1952,[11] they had a volume entitled *The Great Conversation*. The point of this volume was that these great books of Western literature contributed to the discussion of ideas about what makes up the essence of humanity, its great questions and concerns, and that this discussion had been going on since the beginning of humanity.

I have long believed Christians should be involved in this great conversation. And to some degree or other we each *are* involved, in discussions with our friends and family over things that matter to us. The Christian should be involved in two ways: first, as a Christian, and secondly, as a human. That is, in addressing these questions of what life is about—its purpose, the good, why we're here, what matters in life, what real love is—we should be speaking what's on our hearts as individuals, and we should also attempt to think through what being a follower of Jesus requires of us in these areas. Context shapes how we address the questions when we are attempting to describe a "Christian" view of a subject. If we are speaking with fellow Christians, a shared basis of authority makes the language of Christianity acceptable. But if we're in a wider circle, the context is different. Since there is not a shared basis of authority, we speak with those who are on the journey with us but not using the exact same language. As fellow humans we have the right to speak from our own hearts, as does anyone else.

But some of us have the opportunity to bring these ideas into the public arena, with books, articles, essays, poems, music, short stories, painting, films, and more. As films have evolved, they have entered this conversation at various levels. My three goals in film of spreading truth, using the sacred, and building cultural cohesion are attempts to speak my beliefs in the language of film.

I attempted to engage culture with the feature film *To End All Wars*. This is a film that can be used with friends to carry on the great conversation—what life is for, why we're here. The great conversation has always been carried on through great literature, but now it is also being carried on in popular culture through film. Film is the universal language of the day, the Koine Greek of our times. Whether you go to the Philippines, or Turkey, or Argentina, they know, for example, Arnold Schwarzenegger's "Hasta la vista, baby."

Rick Richardson, in *Evangelism Outside the Box*,[12] talks about soul-awakening events we can use to talk with friends about their souls, about the longings, desires, needs they may be ignoring, repressing, satisfying in less than fulfilling ways. This film is a soul-awakening event. It asks questions all of us should be asking of ourselves: What would I do differently if I had the chance to change things in my life? What is life for? How can I overcome adversities to accomplish what I really want? Must I just be a product of my environment? Do I know what I really want in life?

When you go to a Super-Bowl party, there is a lot of fun conversation, with a lot of eating and drinking, commenting on the new commercials, and waiting to see if this year's half-time show will compare with Janet Jackson's year. But as much fun as those events are, they do not lend themselves to discussing the deeper issues of life. In contrast, a movie can do that for us. Going out for coffee with a friend after the movie allows us to reflect on our feelings about it, discuss its issues—for we are in the mood it put us in, at least for this brief period. And we should take advantage of this, for if we talk about things that matter to our friends on such an occasion, then when something important comes up in their lives, the door will have been opened and they will want to talk with us about it—allowing us to be a real friend for them then.

The purpose of a film like *To End All Wars* is to make "the good" look attractive—to make others hunger and thirst for the good and be aware of that hunger. This will greatly impact culture—if we all realize we want the same things.

The use of film is important today in relation to image, story, and reality. The church needs to use the arts more in its presentations, since in this postmodern world image has taken on at least as strong a role as word, if not stronger. We must creatively use image without denigrating or lessening word. We must encourage visual artists in our midst.

In addition, however, when using words we must highlight story rather than just logic as we make our presentations. This is the age of story. The use of story allows truth to come in through the back door. In addition, as the film *To End All Wars* illustrates, film addresses the question of "Is it real?" People in postmodern times want to know if something really works—when they don't automatically accept the authority of the church or the Scriptures, they may consider a first step toward something that seems to work. Read Anne Lamott's story in her *Traveling Mercies*.[13]

The church has come around to engaging with film somewhat late in the game. I want to challenge the church to be that place of community where the person who has just seen a movie can come and be accepted without having to take on a whole subculture to be accepted. My goal was always twofold: to make the movies, but also to have the church be a place of community that accepted the people from outside their subculture. I reasoned, *What did it matter if I made a movie so powerful that people couldn't get out of their seats afterwards because they were so moved and said, "That's what I've been looking for my whole life," if there were no place where they could go on earth to find something like that actually lived out? What did my movie reality matter if it didn't point to a reality not perfect but substantial, as Francis Schaeffer has said?*

So the church must become a seekers' community—accepting those who are seeking a formal faith and making them feel at home. And it must speak the language they speak—seekers must see that the gospel is an answer for the questions and issues of their world.

TO END ALL WARS

The film *To End All Wars,* directed by David L. Cunningham (*Path to 9-11, The Dark Rising*), is the story of the Allies in World War 2 being captured by the Japanese and forced to build the Burma-Siam Railroad, under the most ruthless of conditions, in which thousands were dying of malnutrition, disease, and torture. Starring Kiefer Sutherland (of the TV show *24*), Ciaran McMenamin, and Robert Carlyle (of *Trainspotting, Angela's Ashes, The Full Monty*), the film shows the Allies rising above such horrors to find meaning and purpose.

A film can carry an amazing number of truths. The following are a few ideas I think the film *To End All Wars* raises. Each is worth discussing with someone after the film. The film says that certain things are worth considering:

- Faith is valuable to life.
- There is a spiritual aspect to life.
- Focusing on meeting other people's needs brings personal meaning and hope.
- Sheer selfishness, like hatred, destroys us.
- We must stop and take stock of our life if we want to find true life.
- Life requires that we purposefully appreciate those who are different from us and work to make them feel accepted.

- Freedom is something inside us—not just outside us.
- Each person is of value and life is important.
- We have a responsibility to our neighbor.
- We miss life when we don't forgive.
- At key life junctures we can act in ways that cause us to lose our dignity.
- We can get lost and lose sight of what's truly important in life.
- We can lose our soul.
- And whether or not we let those truths work in our life—whether we strangle or water them—is up to us.

DOCUMENTARIES

A word should be said about documentary films. In examining ideas documentaries can do things feature films can't do. Feature films have to focus on story, whereas documentaries can focus on ideas. But both can be valid ways of carrying on the great conversation and helping to shape culture.

THREE FINAL THOUGHTS

I have three final thoughts. First, as I'm talking to pastors and church leaders, what do I want these people to take away? Do I want them all to go out and make movies? Do I want them to become writers or painters or musicians?

No, if they are afraid of culture, I want them to change their mentality and help change their churches. I want them to relax and enjoy the arts, submit to art, then decide. I want them to make important distinctions as they ponder how to use art. There are two steps. One is for themselves. One is for others. Forget others for a while. Think of how you, personally, can grow from this. If this art is a lie, or is offensive, how will you handle it?

But when we move out from ourselves to think about our responsibilities to the church in relation to the arts, when we make public statements about them, we must be informed and clear in our thinking. We must not overreact or make blanket statements when good thinking requires the use of nuance.

For example, when thinking about the arts, there are three issues to consider separately. There is the artist—how would you treat her if you met? There is the message—what do you think of it? What do you personally learn from it; what would you say to others about it? There is, third, the form, the technique, the medium. Is it enhancing the message, carrying the message, or is it in the way? Is it distasteful? Or uplifting? Is it supposed to be? Is it consistent with the message—well done? Is it good—did it require real skill, thought, planning, craftsmanship?[14]

What do we say about the art (the message and technique) and the artist when we speak about them in a public fashion? Are we gracious? Are we thinking about the seeker of a formal faith, the unbeliever, the visitor who may be living amid the artistic world? Are we alienating him by our approach to culture so that he will never be able to see past our comments to Jesus?

Second, I want to ask the church to encourage youth who want to go into the arts to do so with a sense of high calling, as truth-spreaders. The young artist must see that this is important—and the church must help the artist to do so. The church must acknowledge that this is an important calling in our day: truth-telling through art is crucial. We must encourage those who see this as their calling and not just tell them to become pastors or traditional missionaries. This isn't an either/or.

Truth-telling through art is a very different thing than ministering in a church setting. It calls for real wisdom and fairness. But we need the young person being raised in an MTV world to learn how to communicate amid that world. Or else we have greatly let down the next generation. There is an entire language to be learned, and the church should set aside those who are called to do it, encouraging them, supporting them, inspiring them.

Last, may God be glorified and the world be astonished by how much we love them. That is our greatest tool in changing culture—to actually find myself really liking people and giving our lives for them. Loving them not to "win them to Christ" with some ulterior motive. But loving them because we need them and they need us, and because we are all social creatures who need to talk to someone about issues important to us—even when people know that each of us has biases and agendas. We must come to be people driven to attempt to glorify God by liking others deeply. What a concept. *Solo Gloria Dei.*

NOTES

1. Roy Clouser, *The Myth of Religious Neutrality* (Notre Dame, Ind.: University of Notre Dame Press, 2005).

2. Morris Berman, *The Reenchantment of the World* (Ithaca, N.Y.: Cornell University Press, 1981).

3. Suzi Gablik, *Has Modernism Failed?* (London: Thames & Hudson, 2004); Suzi Gablik, *The Reenchantment of Art* (London: Thames and Hudson, 1995).

4. Let me give an example, as a side note. One person of great interest to me is Christopher Hitchens. I feel kinship with him, like him (though I don't know him personally), and greatly enjoy his writing. But when he writes that "god is not great" to present his own atheism (*God is not Great* (New York: Twelve Books/Hachette, 2007), I can only hope that life gives him what I want it to give me and that he doesn't miss it on the path he chooses. When he gives up God, does he also give up the non-material part of being human? What is his basis for the sacred? I don't understand how he can love poetry and deny the soul. Or I don't understand how he can believe in a soul and not believe in God. He wants so many of the same things I want for the world. I don't think, in other words, that he's against something other than sheer matter being there, nor is he intent on denying his friends the right to derive pleasure and meaning from their faith in God. I think he's just saying that it hasn't made sense to him as of yet. I know he considers some things sacred and not to be tampered with.

However he works it out, I trust he finds something higher than himself to live for that brings him great pleasure in its pursuit—and as a Christian, I can't help but desire that he find the God of T. S. Eliot. Hitchens deserves some blessings—he is a gifted man who has brought many of us joy. But in offering this example, I am saying this is how I approach the stories I tell. I know some may not agree with my perspective in a story, but I see them as friends who will enjoy the experience regardless, since we share the same basic human aspirations and a regard for each other's dignity.

5. Rudolph Otto, *The Idea of the Holy* (London: Oxford University Press, 1923.)

6. Tom Wolfe, *The Painted Word* (New York: Bantam Books), 1975.

7. Consider the 2006 Academy Award winner for Foreign Film, *The Lives of Others*, in which the Communist East German Stasi worker, in overhearing the work of an artist, feels feelings he hasn't experienced before, and it changes his whole worldview.

8. *Image: A Journal of the Arts and Religion*, www.imagejournal.org.

9. Wolfe, Gregory. "The Christian Writer in a Fragmented Culture,"

Image 7 (Fall 1994). Cf. also Gregory Wolfe. "Art, Faith, and the Stewardship of Culture," *Image* 25 (Winter 1999-2000).

10. Gregory Wolfe, "The Christian Writer in a Fragmented Culture," 88.

11. Mortimer J. Adler and Will Hutchens, *Great Books of the Western World* (Encyclopedia Britannica, 1952; 2nd. ed., 1994).

12. Rick Richardson, *Evangelism Outside the Box: New Ways to Help People Experience the Good News* (Downers Grove, Ill.: InterVarsity Press, 2002).

13. Anne Lamott, *Traveling Mercies: Some Thoughts on Faith* (New York: Anchor Books, 2000).

14. Another issue that has been hard for the church to accept is films that are R-rated. The American church doesn't normally endorse those kinds of movies. I understand that. But the church needs to see that the MPAA has a limited way of classifying movies under the current system. The church, then, must make distinctions the MPAA doesn't make. There are different kinds of R-rated movies. If filmmakers want to make films that matter, films that are important, films that make cultural statements, they will realize that often the films that fulfill such goals are R-rated: films such as *Schindler's List, Saving Private Ryan, The Shawshank Redemption, Amistad,* and *Dead Man Walking,* to name just a few.

On the other hand, some PG-13 movies challenge kids to see if they can drive their cars under a moving semi without getting their heads chopped off (*The Fast and the Furious*). Yet Christians will say that we shouldn't attend R-rated movies but movies with a less intense rating are fine. We must go beyond the current rating system. And adults must see the movies affecting society if they want to be able to speak the language of our culture. This is especially true of pastors and leaders. (There are great helps for pastors at such Internet sources of film clips as www.WingClips.com.)

Chapter 7

To Know and Be Known: Evangelicals and Interfaith Dialogue

Marvin R. Wilson

Dr. Marvin R. Wilson is the Harold J. Ockenga Professor of Biblical and Theological Studies at Gordon College, Wenham, Massachussetts. He holds the B.A. from Wheaton College (Ill.), the M.Div. from Gordon-Conwell Theological Seminary, the M.A. and Ph.D. from Brandeis University. Wilson's teaching speciality at Gordon College is Old Testament, Jewish Studies, and the Hebraic origins of Christianity. Wilson's college teaching career spans nearly five decades since he joined the Barrington College (R.I.) faculty in 1963 before becoming part of the Gordon faculty from 1971 to the present.

An active writer in the field of Christian-Jewish relations, Wilson has authored dozens of articles in scholarly journals and general religious periodicals. His widely used textbook, *Our Father Abraham: Jewish Roots of the Christian Faith* (Eerdmans, 1989) is currently in its twenty-second printing. In addition, he has co-edited four books on Evangelical-Jewish relations with Rabbi A. James Rudin, including *Evangelicals and Jews in Conversation* (Baker, 1978); *Evangelicals and Jews in an Age of Pluralism* (Baker, 1984); and *A Time to Speak: The Evangelical-Jewish Encounter* (Eerdmans, 1987).

Wilson is the primary scholar of an award-winning television documentary, "Jews & Christians: A Journey of Faith" (2000), a program seen on more than 200 PBS stations nationwide, and screened at the National Press Club. He has also served as consultant to the documentary, *Three Faiths, One God: Judaism, Christianity, Islam*, and authored the extensive study guide to this two-hour public television program.

Marvin Wilson has made twenty-five extensive study tours of Israel and the Middle East. He has lectured widely in synagogues and has addressed a number of prestigious international gatherings of Jewish and Christian leaders. Wilson has co-chaired four national conferences of evangelicals and Jews. He has also addressed a variety of "Abrahamic Faith" conferences organized to bring Jews, Muslims, and Christians together for interfaith discussion.

Wilson has received many awards and honors for his work in interfaith relations. These include recognition from the Anti-Defamation League, the B'Nai B'rith, the Jewish Federation, the Holocaust Center of Greater Boston, the International Christian Embassy Jerusalem, and International Excellence in the Media. Wilson has also been cited by the Jewish community for his bridge-building work between evangelicals and Jews through his creative field trip course on Modern Judaism.

A pivotal command for Christians is this one: "Love your neighbor as yourself." Moses established this teaching, and Jesus re-enforced it, declaring that love of God and neighbor is the mega-commandment for his followers (Lev. 19:18; Mark 12:28-34).

Every concerned and culturally alert generation of Christians must keep asking, "Who is my neighbor?" There is a good possibility one's neighbor may be a Jew or a Muslim, especially in the cities and suburbs. Next to Christianity, Judaism and Islam are the two largest world religions found in America. How many evangelical Christians really know their neighbors, especially when they espouse a faith tradition different than their own? And how many Jews and Muslims have been sensitively encouraged to cross the interfaith divide to really get to know evangelical Christians? Is it not presumptuous for a Christian to claim love of neighbors despite making little effort to know and understand those of different faith traditions living nearby? Is it possible to fulfill Jesus' command by choosing to remain largely aloof from one's neighbor and uninformed about the neighbor's religious beliefs and practices? Do Christians have an obligation to build bridges of understanding and dynamic engagement with those of other faiths? In heaven, will there be any credit for avoiding the other?

My conviction and experience is this: if Christians are *to be known*, they must also *know*. We cannot genuinely love one we do not know. To "know" is not to confront abruptly, then dismiss quickly. Knowing someone implies a process; it is not a "bump and run." Indeed, to know, as I use this term in the context of interfaith relations, is to grow in understanding and appreciation of the other through respectful conversation and shared experiences leading to mutual enrichment and trust. In this chapter, I explore lessons I have learned from my own personal journey of more than forty years as an evangelical venturing into the world of knowing others through interreligious conversation.

SEARCH FOR HEBRAIC ROOTS

I was raised in a Christian home, attended a Christian high school, and graduated from an evangelical Christian college and seminary. Following seminary, my university training was in Semitic and Mediterranean Studies—the languages, history, and culture of the Bible world. I began my teaching career in the early 1960s at an evangelical Christian college in New England. At the time, I thought I understood the history of the Jewish people, biblical literature, and how it applied to life today. As I look back, however, I realize how shallow my understanding was, especially concerning biblical Judaism and the last two thousand years of Jewish history. In addition, I soon discovered that what was lacking in my own personal life was actually a rather ubiquitous Christian problem, one prevalent throughout the church.

One of the hallmarks of historic, classic Christianity is belief in Jesus as Messiah and Son of God. This point however has caused division and hostility between Christians and Jews for nearly two thousand years. It remains an impasse which, humanly speaking, only God himself can ultimately bridge.

The consequence of this Christian-Jewish impasse left many Christians believing that Jews have everything to learn from them but Christians have little or nothing to learn from Jews. For centuries, many in the church were mainly taught to feel sorry for Jews because they had missed the boat, theologically speaking. In the Christian scheme, Jews were often viewed as objects to confront and win over to the Christian side for the sake of the "Gospel." Christians, on the other hand, typically saw themselves as having no ongoing need of Jews and Judaism.

Such limited thinking doubtless influenced the general malaise, passivity, and indifference of Christians toward Jews at the time of the Holocaust. Thus, because the church tended to view Judaism as a defective and "incomplete" faith, Christian teachers largely refused to take Jews and Judaism all that seriously. Rather, for many, the church had replaced Israel; the church was the new and true people of God. Hence Judaism was basically viewed as a theological cadaver, an antiquated, legalistic religion, a mere springboard to Christianity. So, once Christianity was born, the importance of Jews and Judaism had every reason to fall off the Christian radar screen.

I had, in general, inherited and been influenced by this view of Jews and Judaism. During my first semester as a full time college professor, I remember how frustrated I was. Students would ask me questions about Judaism and Jewish-Christian relations I could not answer intelligently. I was woefully unprepared because my Christian teachers had never given any serious attention to the Jewish roots of the Christian faith and to understanding the importance of post-biblical Judaism.

I still remember many of those frustrating questions. Here are a few examples: If the temple was destroyed in A.D. 70, and animal sacrifices ceased, how do Jews today seek atonement of sin? When Jews hold a Passover seder today, why do Jews eat chicken or fish, rather than lamb? Why do traditional Jews usually prefer Tuesday for their wedding day? Why does a bridegroom smash a glass at a Jewish wedding? In the book of Genesis, if Jacob and Joseph were both embalmed, why are Jews today usually opposed to embalming the dead? What is the relation of Jewish ritual immersion to early Christian baptism? If Paul, a Pharisaic Jew from the tribe of Benjamin and a student of the Jewish sage Gamaliel, held to the teaching of "original sin," why do modern rabbis seem to oppose this teaching (cf. Phil. 3:5; Acts 22:3; Rom. 5:12-19)?

My frustration with the questions above, and others like them, soon started me on a search to help fill this yawning gap in my education. Before long, I came to conclude that most evangelical Christians tend to score quite high in their knowledge of Jews and Judaism from Abraham to Jesus; their knowledge is generally very low, however, in the same subject areas from Jesus to the present. Christians tend to have little understanding of how Judaism, from the end of the first century onward, began to be reformulated, resulting in a reinterpretation of many aspects of biblical Judaism. In the Christian community this ignorance and blind spot has led to naiveté, misunderstanding, and distortion of contemporary Judaism by Christians everywhere. Indeed, it has often resulted in painful caricatures and ignorant, gross violations of the Seventh Commandment: "You shall not give false testimony against your neighbor" (Exod. 20:16).

OVERCOMING FEAR AND LEARNING TO LISTEN

The first few years of college teaching, I became increasingly concerned with the question of why Christians seemed so indifferent and unconcerned about Christian-Jewish relations and the Hebraic roots of the Church's faith. It just did not compute. The very foundation of the Christian faith came from the Jewish people. Why do so many Christians seem to care less? The church's Scriptures, its theology, ethics, spirituality, and its understanding of history, social justice, and worship all came from Israel. Indeed, Gentile believers were "grafted into Israel"; Paul warned them not to be arrogant or triumphal, for the root of the olive tree (Israel) supported Gentiles, not Gentiles the root (Rom. 11:18-20).

In light of these life-changing gifts of the Jews, I concluded that the only acceptable attitude of Gentile believers toward Jews was one of indebtedness, thankfulness, and appreciation. The more I studied, however, the more I became convinced that a main cause of the Holocaust was that anti-Judaism and anti-Semitism were allowed to fester in and around the church from the early Christian centuries to the twentieth. The church had received its spiritual heritage from the Jews. Instead of esteeming that inheritance, the offspring had turned against the parent. I wondered why the church, a people who had received so much from the Jewish community, could be so seemingly insensitive and uncaring.

Early on, I came to realize the evangelical and Jewish communities really did not know each other. Evangelicals and Jews passed like ships in the night. For the most part, Jews feared evangelicals because Jews saw them mainly as heavy-handed proselytizers, a people who only knew how to confront Jews about where they had fallen short on theology in general and the Messiah in particular. Sadly, some Jews rather crassly described the evangelical mindset as having but one goal: stealing Jewish souls.

Especially since the 1950s, many Jews had become increasingly wary of the U.S. evangelical movement, particularly its alleged goal of "Christianizing" America. Few Jews, however, had actually experienced personal dialogue with evangelical leaders, so they largely lacked an appreciation for the diversity of the evangelical movement and its intellectual depth.

A major consequence of this lack of social interaction and friendship-building was pejorative stereotyping of evangelicals. I have heard Jews caricature the evangelical as little more than a missionary seeking to prey on uninformed Jews. An evangelical-Jewish encounter is often viewed with trepidation because Jews fear it will be a one-way street, and they resent the notion of being targeted. Often when Jews have encountered evangelicals, Jews have expressed fear and defensiveness, worrying some unpleasant confrontation will result. Interfaith events can result in genuine dialogue and an opportunity to develop positive friendships, or they can be distasteful and even repulsive experiences. Meanwhile sometimes Jews have taken the offensive against evangelicals. Over the years, I have personally witnessed some Jews express hostility, challenge, or even outright belligerency toward evangelicals.

Either way, however, every situation I have witnessed has left me with the conviction that we must find a better way. We have to talk. There is such a thing as respectful conversation, not a war of words. We can learn to disagree without being disagreeable. Let me share two illustrations concerning our need to listen to each other to overcome stereotypes and fear.

Many years ago, I was asked to address a regional gathering of Conservative rabbis on the theme of "Evangelical-Jewish Relations." In my talk, held at a Conservative synagogue, I sought to define evangelicalism as a movement and to explain why the Jewish community should not be suspicious of all evangelicals. After my presentation, during the question-and-answer session, an influential younger rabbi, new to the Boston area, stood to reprimand me. He had never seen me before, but he alleged that I was a deceiver who did not know what I was talking about when it came to evangelicals. He charged I was really a "wolf in sheep's clothing." Needless to say, this experience left me shaken.

I did receive comfort and encouragement, however, from three local rabbi friends. They knew me well. We had been working in interfaith activities together for several years. These rabbis insisted on walking me out to my car after the event. Each apologized to me for the display of anger directed at me by their colleague in the rabbinate, a man who had never seen or worked with me before. The whole experience convinced me that we should not use labels to prejudge or stereotype others. Instead of relying on preconceived notions in the abstract, through personal engagement we should seek to know, and build trust with, the other. That requires time and does not permit rushing to judgment by relying on hearsay.

My second illustration involves a painful learning experience I had in the late 1970s; it was an encounter I will never forget. I had personally invited a local rabbi to address a Bible class of evangelicals studying the Book of Isaiah. The class wanted to hear a Jewish perspective on the Suffering Servant of Isaiah, chapter 53. The rabbi felt some trepidations about coming when I contacted him. But I also had my doubts whether it would work. Yes, the subject was controversial for a rabbi to address. But I also was concerned about one newly professed Christian in the group whose personality tended to be arrogant, confrontational, and pushy.

The rabbi came to make his presentation as guest teacher; he left shaken and angry. Why? At the conclusion of his lecture, the pushy student decided not to ask a question of the rabbi but rather to make a speech so he could "witness" publicly, using the event as an occasion to press his own theological agenda on the rabbi. Unfortunately, he came across to the rabbi more like a prosecuting attorney than one truly interested in hearing the rabbi's interpretation of the prophecy of Isaiah. As the rabbi was being confronted by this unexpected tirade, he became increasingly impatient and agitated. Suddenly, the rabbi turned toward me and said, "You're a *momser* [literally a "bastard," and by extension, an untrustworthy and detestable person]. You tricked me!" You evangelicals really don't want to hear my view of Isaiah 53; you only brought me here to put me on trial for my faith as a Jew!" I felt the pain of betrayal in the rabbi's voice.

It took me five years to reestablish communication and begin to restore that relationship. I was still determined, however, to pursue respectful conversation. In the end, I am happy to say it worked. In the years that followed, the rabbi and I continued to deepen our friendship until the rabbi suddenly became ill and then passed away. Before he died, however, he left instructions that he wanted me, an evangelical, to be one of the speakers at his memorial service. At the service I shared how the rabbi and I had, through pain, grown in understanding of each other and of our joint love for the Word of God.

EVANGELICALS IN THE SYNAGOGUE

My first few years of college teaching had left me convinced that book knowledge about Jews and Judaism was not enough. If there was to be a decrease in the knowledge gap, there also had to be personal, long-term interaction with the Jewish community. At first, I invited local rabbis to lecture in some of my classes. It helped to put "an address and a face" on things we were studying in class. Often these lectures were sponsored by the Jewish Chautauqua Society. For the most part, the lectures were beneficial. But they did more than inform. The physical presence of a rabbi in class began to break down the communication barrier and mysterious wall which seemed to separate us. Students could ask questions of the rabbi in the familiarity and security of their own Christian classroom. Lasting friendships with the Jewish community began to be established.

This form of education about Jews and Judaism raised a question for me still not resolved: the Jewish community is willing to sponsor its scholar-teachers to go into Christian institutions to teach on virtually any requested theme about Judaism and the "Jewish story." Will the day ever come when the Christian community makes its scholars available to speak in the Jewish community and at its own expense? Would the Jewish community ever be open to this, or is this stretching interfaith too far?

Within a few months, one of the Chautauqua-sponsored rabbis who had spoken several times to my classes called me. He asked if I would be willing to read a section from the Torah (Deut. 28) at his installation service at a nearby synagogue. I told him I would be honored to do so. It is always a privilege to read Scripture. The occasion proved to be joyful, yet sobering. The event began to open my eyes to the possibility of Christians learning from Jews, and participating with Jews, in the synagogue. I took a measure of encouragement from the observation of Martin Buber, late Jewish biblical scholar: "We [Jews and Christians] share a Book, and that is no small thing." I could see some real learning potential through onsite visits to synagogues. But I wondered how Jews would respond to a large group of non-Jewish visitors. I was curious to find out, so I decided I needed a course to be the vehicle for engaging in this type of off-campus learning.

The next fall I developed a new course. I called it Modern Jewish Culture, a title that has remained to this day. From the beginning, the course has proved to be a sort of potpourri on "Everything I wish I had been taught about Jews and Judaism—but was not." Its main components, however, have included the beliefs and practices of Judaism, the Jewish roots of the Christian faith, and the history of Christian-Jewish relations. I want my students to be familiar with the similarities and differences between Judaism and Christianity as well as to grasp why interfaith relations are important and how they are implemented. I was determined that learning must not be limited to textbooks and lectures. Students also had to learn from, and interact with, Jews in situ. To do so required field trips, a decision I am very glad to have made.

To date, I have made with my Christian students over four hundred course-related field trips into the Jewish community. These visits have significantly shaped our perceptions of Jews and Judaism. We have visited worship services at Orthodox, Conservative, Reform, and Hasidic houses of worship. We have celebrated Jewish holidays, including Rosh Hashanah, Succot,

Simchat Torah, Purim, Pesach, and Shavuot. We have attended
Yom HaShoah (Holocaust Commemoration) gatherings; visited
Jewish day schools, Jewish funeral homes, Jewish historical
sites; and attended dozens of lectures and interfaith events at
Jewish community centers. We have spent dozens of hours in
local synagogues discussing Judaism and Christianity with rabbis, either before or after services. We continue to be graciously
received.

EXTENDING HOSPITALITY IN WORSHIP

But do Jews feel as welcome and comfortable in evangelical
churches as Christians typically do in most synagogues? From
the Christian perspective, many churchgoers would quickly say
yes, quite unaware of how de-judaized the church has become
over the centuries! From the Jewish perspective, however, Jews
often feel like fish out of water. To be comfortable within a
church is not an easy matter. Some Jewish leaders openly dis-
courage visiting churches, or they express extreme caution about
this idea. There are historical, theological, practical, and even
symbolic reasons for this point of view. If Jews ever do enter a
church, many Jews see themselves doing so only as visitors or
observers of a service, never as participants.

In contemporary society, marriages, funerals, and other rites
of passage do often bring Jews into churches. In addition, the
high rate of intermarriage, and the consequent expectations
placed on the Jewish partner of an interfaith couple, have increasingly brought many Jews within churches. Many separatis-
tic, traditional Jews, however, tend to abide by at least two un-
written instructions concerning Christians: (1) never enter a
church; and (2) never discuss theology with a Christian. In addition to such restrictive guidelines, occasionally Orthodox Jews
have been known to protest and to use physical force to ban their
own from taking part in an interfaith event. This is an expression
of a "closed" Judaism, unlike the more "open" modern Orthodox, who have made certain adaptations to the realities of contemporary society.

I will share one interfaith illustration from an experience I
had with closed Orthodoxy. In the 1990s, I was invited to be one
of the Christian speakers at an international interfaith confer-

ence at the Jerusalem Convention Center. Other Christian speakers on the program included the Archbishop of Canterbury and a Catholic cardinal from Germany named Joseph Ratzinger (but a decade later elected Pope, assuming the title Benedict XVI). Before the conference began, the Chief Rabbi of Israel appeared on television and told Israeli Jews to protest the event and to warn others not to attend. The Chief Rabbi's position was that Jews were a majority religion in Israel, and so Jews had no reason meeting with or talking to those of another faith. The same day on which the archbishop, the cardinal, and I lectured, dozens of Orthodox Israeli Jews waged a sitdown protest, barricading the entrance to the hall of the Convention Center. I had never witnessed before in America this kind of protest of an interfaith event. I was glad when the Jerusalem police removed the protestors and allowed the conference to proceed.

Fortunately, not all Jews take the position that to enter a church, or to meet with Christians in their house of worship or even in another "neutral" venue, is to condone or approve all the teachings and activities of the other. If that were the case in America, Christian-Jewish relations would not have made the enormous strides they have since World War II. While many Jews are still somewhat tentative about entering the doors of a church to be present for a service of Christian worship, I have heard different responses from two rabbi friends of mine. I will briefly comment on each. The first rabbi, Orthodox in his identity, explains to me that he has no difficulty with certain aspects of the Christian worship service. For example, he says that from a Jewish theological perspective, there is not a line in the Lord's Prayer (Matt. 6:9-13) with which he disagrees. He says, in principle, he could pray these words of Jewish origin with a group of Christians, but he chooses *not* to do so. According to this rabbi, the reason he will not pray the Lord's Prayer is primarily "symbolic." That is, it boils down mainly to a matter of outward, social Jewish identity. In the rabbi's view, if he were to stand beside Christians in a church and pray a prayer coming from the Christian Gospels, this act could easily send the wrong message. So the rabbi chooses to abstain, even from the more "Jewish" parts of a Christian service.

Another rabbi, a friend whose view I also respect, is from the Conservative movement. He takes a different position. Personally, he is open to "selective participation" in church services. For example, this rabbi has told me of an evangelical church where he has a close relation with the pastor. The pastor and church members study Hebrew with the rabbi and sometimes join in services at his synagogue. However, the rabbi and his congregants are occasionally present at the church across the street. The rabbi states that he does this because he is sincerely open to learn from Christians, a point few rabbis will admit to—all the more so in public. In the rabbi's words, "We Jews don't know everything about God; we have a lot to learn from this church in town." The rabbi further emphasizes, "These [Christian] people have a spontaneous expression of spirituality which is moving; their prayers are natural and from the heart, and their music is alive."

MOVING FROM DIALOGUE TOWARD "TRIALOGUE"

Christianity began as a movement within Judaism. For the first two decades of the church, the only way one could be part of the church was by being a Jew. From one perspective, the church is the outgrowth of an inhouse Jewish debate. By the middle of the first century, however, the church had opened its doors to any believer, Jew or non-Jew. In light of this common origin, of the three Abrahamic monotheistic religions, Christianity will always remain closest to Judaism. Islam, on the other hand, while revising portions of the Jewish and Christian Scriptures, claims the Qur'an is a new prophetic revelation. In Islamic teaching, this Word of God was recited in the seventh century by Allah, through the angel Gabriel, to the prophet Muhammed.

Since the beginning of Islam, both Judaism and Christianity said no to any additional prophetic voices. All three religions, however, do share common themes, though each faith tradition nuances these concepts and practices somewhat differently. For example, each believes in God as Creator and Judge, One to whom adherents daily submit their wills and seek mercy and forgiveness through the medium of prayer. In addition, each religious community lays claim to Abraham as father, each holds Moses in high honor as a prophet, each is avowedly monotheistic, each passionately opposes idolatry and false gods, each is committed to the practice of social justice and care of the poor. All three hold to an afterlife of reward or punishment.

For many years, I essentially ignored Islam. But a seed had been planted during my graduate school days. I had studied some Arabic in graduate school, and my dissertation committee was comprised of a mix of three scholars from different religious traditions: a Jew, a Muslim, and a Christian. As a university student, not unlike most American Christians at that time, I thought Islam was a religion mainly confined to the Middle East, Indonesia, and parts of Africa. How limited and wrong-headed *that* thinking was! Today, Islam is on the rise around the globe, and in American society its presence is increasing rapidly. New mosques are being constructed in the cities and suburbs of America. With greater frequency than ever, Muslims, Jews, and Christians run into each other in the supermarket, in public schools, at town meetings, in neighborhoods, and on the soccer and Little League fields.

I believe Christians and Jews now need to expand interfaith conversation cautiously and thoughtfully from dialogue to "trialogue." It is important to include moderate Muslim voices for reasons I explain below. Polls indicate many American Christians and Jews have unfavorable views toward Muslims and the religion of Islam. If I listened to these surveys, I would probably not advocate that the evangelical community build bridges with Muslims. But my thinking has been strongly influenced in recent years through my being the evangelical participant of five different trialogues held at a variety of educational institutions.

Why should evangelicals be talking to Muslims? First, we should be in conversation because the church has always borne witness to all continents and all peoples. In addition, the American religious landscape is rapidly changing. We can no longer ignore the fact our next-door neighbor may belong to the Muslim community. At the end of the day, people of the Abrahamic faith communities need to do more than criticize and compete with the other; they must listen to each other. It is all too easy to focus on misguided, radical, or extremist expressions of any faith in an attempt to invalidate or destroy that faith. There are good, upright, and exemplary people—as well as those who are not—in any faith community. We must not define a faith solely by those whose radical actions contradict the basic historic tenets of that faith, especially tenets embracing social justice, pursuit of peace, and compassion toward others.

138 / MUTUAL TREASURE

If it were valid to define a faith based on its worst expression, then Christianity could be invalidated and rather quickly dismissed due to the actions of the Crusaders or the collaboration of Christians with Nazis to exterminate Jews. In my view, with full integrity, without coercion, and without theological compromise, each Abrahamic faith must make every effort possible to understand and communicate with the other. Evangelicals are called not to be isolationists but a community of Christians who believe they have a biblical mandate to love their neighbors, on every side, and respectfully share their lives and spiritual journey.

Evangelicals cannot be ostriches hiding in fear of the other. Judeophobia, Islamophobia, and xenophobia have never been a hallmark of the church (cf. Rom. 12:13). We must do more than demonize, denounce, or defame the other from the secure confines of our evangelical pulpits and inhouse Bible studies. Christians cannot demand respect; it must be earned. Not by dominating others, but by first listening and then entering focused, respectful conversations, evangelicals will be able to build meaningful friendships rooted in kind and loving service to others. For evangelicals, interfaith relations cannot work without unconditional love for others and a commitment to reconcile as far as one can reconcile—without theological compromise.

TOWARD REFINING INTERFAITH CONVERSATION

Continued progress in interfaith relations cannot be taken for granted. There are still barriers to break down and much yet to learn about the other. As I have emphasized, if evangelicals are to be known, they must also make a sincere effort to know the other. No friendship can genuinely prosper if some partners impose their own way, insisting, "It's about us; come and learn solely about us; we are everything!" It does not work that way. Friendships are two-way streets. Friends value honest sharing. If a relationship is to grow and prosper, there has to be giving, not simply receiving. In interfaith relations, respectful conversation must replace confrontation, dynamic engagement replace strident badgering, and dialogue replace monologue.

From the time I first entered the world of interreligious dialogue, I have learned many valuable lessons through reading, listening, attentively watching, and personally participating. Accordingly, I offer a number of guidelines or rules of thumb for evangelicals to consider to move the dialogue to a greater level of maturity and productivity.

First, we must be committed to make gradual progress in small steps, rather than through quick giant strides. Often the process is more like being on a seemingly unending journey rather than realizing we have suddenly arrived home. Evangelical-Jewish dialogue is a long-term venture. But it can be like a roller coaster; it has its ups and downs. Sometimes we take three steps forward and two back. Patience is required, for there is often a newness and strangeness to our dialogue partners and their faith orientations—as they in turn will experience with us. It takes a commitment of time over many months—even years—to come to know the other and build trust.

There is no room for preemptive "turf claiming" here. "Love is patient" and "endures all things" (cf. 1 Cor. 13:4, 7). Inaccuracies and misperceptions of the other cannot be overcome overnight. After nearly two thousand years of considerable animosity, conflict, and avoidance, only in the decades after World War II have we begun to see some progress toward rapprochement between us. Therefore we must always be reminded that when Christians and Jews come together, history is on the table. Sadly, Christians especially carry a lot of baggage due to a long history of misunderstanding, hatred, and contempt.

My second guideline has to do with the style with which evangelicals conduct dialogue. Evangelicals must first commit ourselves to listen, then speak. Listening is a godly virtue; some would even call it the ultimate form of humility. When the time comes to speak, evangelicals must always speak truth—as we personally have come to know and understand this—in love (Eph. 4:15). There will be times when evangelicals and Jews disagree. When evangelicals disagree, we must learn to disagree sincerely, yet graciously. Such is a Spirit-filled art, not something which comes by intensive training from a debate coach. The style and demeanor of evangelicals should always be one of humility and modesty, especially regarding truth claims. Evangelicals understand that the truth we proclaim is already the truth which has sought us out. Thus our attitude and posture is not one of triumphalism, assertiveness, showmanship, or arrogance. Rather, evangelicals speak as "beggars" telling other beggars where we have found bread.

A necessary prerequisite for effective dialogue is the willingness of evangelicals to learn from Jews. Thus there is no place for pride, aggressiveness, or hubris. Evangelicals are servants, not masters. Evangelicals will seek no compromise regarding our theological non-negotiables. But we must be committed to display integrity, uprightness, and the highest moral principles in our discussions. We must learn to humbly submit our views for discussion at the dialogue table, not pontificate in a spirit of self-importance. Too often in centuries past, for example, Christians have spoken for Jews rather than allowing Jews to speak for themselves. There is therefore a reticence and reserve required by Christians in dialogue. Indeed, Paul admonishes us to "in humility consider others better than yourselves" (Phil. 2:3). It is contradictory to say one has experienced grace yet does not display graciousness; has experienced mercy yet is unmerciful and judgmental; has experienced love yet is unloving.

Third, evangelicals believe the Spirit of God is active everywhere. The Spirit primarily works relationally in the lives of people, guiding, teaching, comforting, empowering, and convicting. The Spirit has a special redemptive role in the lives of believers. But God's Presence may also be discerned in the lives of those outside the church; God providentially works far beyond the categories theologians often confine God to. The so-called "common grace" of God is everywhere active in the world. If God can describe Nebuchadnezzar, a pagan king, as "my servant," and Persian King Cyrus, "my anointed," God indeed may be present and active in interfaith activities which are God-honoring. When caring for the poor and hungry, justice, righteousness, reconciliation, goodness, kindness, and peacemaking are displayed in this world, such may be potent signs of God's presence and the manifestation of God's will for humankind.

The starkness of a purely theological starting point for dialogue, if it fails to include also the relational dimensions emphasized in a more pneumatologically focused paradigm, is likely to minimize dynamic practical concern for the other. Unfortunately, exclusivism has often led to isolationism. God, to be sure, is at work in relationships. Theology is not simply propositional; it also has incarnational and dynamic dimensions. Our partners in dialogue can be too quickly dismissed because they fail to measure up to the standard of our theological yardstick.

In interfaith dialogue, however, when looking into the face of our partner, we may see the image of God (Gen. 1:26). As divine image bearers, Christians and Jews remind us that every human life has significance, dignity, and value to the Almighty. Though marred by sin and finiteness, each person reflects a divine likeness. Therefore, it is imperative when evangelicals come to the dialogue table that we show respect, honor, appropriate regard, and consideration toward our partners. Agreement on everything is not necessary; a willing spirit is. We can sincerely believe others are wrong and still respect them, show unconditional love for them, and do good to them. The dialogue table is no place for the "last word." Only God is absolute; only God has the right to judge with finality and perfect knowledge.

A fourth guideline is for evangelicals to remember that presently we know only "in part" (1 Cor. 13:12). What cannot be fully harmonized or reconciled in this life must be left in the hands of the Ultimate Reconciler. In the meantime, these issues and tensions cannot be resolved by crusaders, jihadists, or political forces aimed at militantly furthering one people's religious agenda at the expense of another's. The diverse religious communities of any nation will have their disagreements among themselves and among other nations.

In that vein, suicide bombing is never an acceptable expression of protest. Why? Every human being, right or wrong, has been created in God's likeness. Whatever intentionally and randomly seeks to destroy innocent human lives defaces God's creation and so diminishes the divine Presence in the world. The evangelical acknowledges a different type of conflict and a different means for conflict resolution. Ultimate resolution of conflict comes not by force or power but by the gentle persuasion and yielding of the human heart and will, voluntarily moved in submission to the Almighty. Our "weapons" are not earthly but of the realm of the Spirit (Zech. 4:6; Eph. 6:10-18).

My fifth observation is this: In seeking a better way through respectful conversation, evangelicals must realize we may often have to be satisfied with incomplete answers and partial agreement on various interfaith discussion points. In Scripture, truth is often indirectly or obliquely approached through the use of parables, analogies, or the answering of a question with another question. In certain evangelical circles there is a stark either/or approach to truth, a mindset which demands coming to full agreement and closure on every issue *now*! In Jewish-Christian relations, as in the interpretation of a large part of Scripture itself, there will always be ambiguities, loose ends, and contrasting schools of thought.

The differences between Christianity and Islam tend to be even greater due to Islam's claim to a new revelation, the Qur'an, in the seventh century A.D. But if agreement on everything is a necessity for dialogue, then there can be no dialogue. The main prerequisite for dialogue is to come to the table with the right of self-definition and to grant that same right to others around the table. Depending on the agenda, this will lead to a mutual search for understanding and discovery of truth, wherever it lies. Though evangelicals first seek answers from biblical sources, we also acknowledge the importance of tradition, reason, and experience in working out the implications of our faith.

Evangelicals must acknowledge that a partial agreement on the discussion of what is truth and the will of God is better than total rejection of an entire system. There must be the ability to live with dialectical tensions, paradoxes, and incongruities. Dialogue will not work if we must be "right" on every issue. We have to listen in relation to every issue—and listen with a teachable spirit. All humans must acknowledge that we are fallible, far from omniscient. If the sole purpose of talking is to get an "opponent" to concede rather than to see and understand another perspective, then we are not engaging in dialogue. What we do with the discussion and evidence presented in dialogue is a personal matter. A successful dialogue is respectful conversation, not relentless argument; a willingness to hear the depths of the pain of another and be heard; the discovery that God loves honest questions and is pleased with those who seek answers.

Many evangelical critics of interreligious dialogue fear such a venture is really reductionism. That is, they claim such an encounter is aimed at reducing each faith to its lowest common denominator so a symbiotic, homogenized, generic religion will emerge. In my view, this is totally false and a misunderstanding of the word *dialogue*. This is not about relativism or theological capitulation. I, along with most other evangelical Christians I know, am fully committed to historic Christian beliefs for specific reasons. Evangelical Christian identity is not a matter of physical birth but of scripturally born convictions. We are called to know what we believe and why we believe it. In evangelical Christianity, the preexistent Word, the deity of Jesus, his sinless life, atoning death, bodily resurrection, and second coming as King of kings and Lord of lords (see Rev. 17:14; 19:16), are among the classic, central beliefs which distinguish Christianity among the Abrahamic faiths. And it will always be that way. A Christianity which becomes theologically diluted loses its distinctiveness and ceases to be an authentic expression of that faith.

To be known, one must first know. The twenty-first century will reveal if American evangelical Christians are willing to accept the current cultural challenge to reach out to further bridge the interfaith divide.

Chapter 8

Conversations on Homosexuality as a Quest to Love Enemy Prejudices

Michael A. King

Michael A. King, Telford, Pennsylvania, a writer, publisher, and ordained minister, has been a pastor in congregations large and small, most recently at Spring Mount (Pa.) Mennonite Church (1997-2008). In addition to many articles, King has had published such books as *Fractured Dance: Gadamer and Mennonite Conflict Over Homosexuality* (Pandora Press U.S., 2001), *Preaching About Life in a Threatening World* (co-authored with Ron Sider, Westminster Press, 1987), and *Trackless Wastes and Stars to Steer By: Christian Identity in a Homeless Age* (Herald Press, 1990).

A theorist of communication with a Ph.D. from Temple University, an M.Div. from Eastern Baptist (now Palmer) Theological Seminary, and a B.A. in Bible and Philosophy from Eastern Mennonite University, King is editor of *DreamSeeker Magazine*; of *Stumbling Toward a Genuine Conversation on Homosexuality* (Cascadia, 2007); and (with David B. Greiser) of *Anabaptist Preaching: A Conversation Between Pulpit, Pew, and Bible* (Cascadia, 2004).

L oving enemy prejudices. In this case, that entails moving from homosexuality as an issue to wage war over to homosexuality as an arena for mutual learning. This chapter records my transition from one to the other in hopes of inspiring others to their own unique yet comparable transitions.

Homosexuality as cause for battle seems a dominant cultural and church emphasis. I functioned within it myself into the 1980s. But then, with heightening intensity in the 1990s and beyond, I began to explore alternatives. That exploration led to my publishing a dissertation on the topic, publishing a book based on the dissertation,[1] as editor pulling together on the basis of my earlier theorizing a Winter 2006 special issue of *DreamSeeker Magazine* on "Toward a Genuine Conversation on Homosexuality,"[2] then in 2007 editing and releasing *Stumbling Toward a Genuine Conversation on Homosexuality,*[3] based on but tripling the number of pages devoted to the *DreamSeeker Magazine* conversation. Treating that exploration as a case study, this chapter reports on roots of the exploration, details the exploration, and summarizes learnings.

Much of this book investigates how Christians might more constructively engage members of our larger culture. This chapter sharpens the focus particularly to successes and failures in Mennonite conversations on homosexuality. Nevertheless, I think and hope the theories and applications I explore here can be pertinent as well to broader engagements with culture. The heartbeat of my approach is Jesus' teaching to love enemies. So my passion comes from my Christian faith. But I theorize that passion through Hans-Georg Gadamer, whose philosophical hermeneutics are applicable to but also transcend explicitly Christian perspectives.

In addition, even as many cultural conversation partners may be secular, increasingly cultural conversations involve not Christians versus those of other faiths or no faith; they involve other Christians. This means that, ever more often these days, to learn how to engage culture constructively is to learn how to engage constructively other Christians in our broader cultural conversation with whom we may disagree.

Meanwhile this volume's authors describe a range of strategies for engaging culture. Many chapters focus on face-to-face conversations. Others explore more impersonal means, whether essays, books, films, or other works of art. This chapter tends toward the latter category, reporting particularly on conversation more as a sequence of publications then face-to-face interaction.

In so doing, my case study may highlight contributions and limitations of various forms of communication. My project is encouraging published conversation on homosexuality. Yet within the published conversation, as noted below, some authors see face-to-face interaction as more do be desired. My own conclusion is that different conversation strategies fit different circumstances. Thus my search is less to establish a particular form of conversation as preferable and more to tease out ingredients of genuine conversation wherever they may be found.

My investment in published conversations is not due to seeing them as superior to other forms of communication. Rather, in relation to homosexuality at least, no form of conversation seems to have developed consistent ability to move from battle to mutual learning. No face-to-face conversations I have been able to observe—including those studied and analyzed for my dissertation, see below—have been entirely successful. At the same time, I happen as a writer, editor, and publisher to be in a position particularly to encourage published conversation. My goal then has been within this arena to seek ways to encourage and at least minimally to model moving from battle to genuine conversation—while concluding that here also success remains at best mixed.

GADAMERIAN ROOTS OF THE JOURNEY

Turning now to the specifics of my project, let me start with an overview of the "effective history" that produced the "prejudices"[4] that delimited my "horizon"[5] of understanding. Here I am using the vocabularly of Gadamer, who spent much of the twentieth century developing his "philosophical hermeneutics" and whose thought has played a key role in my quest for how we might treat homosexuality as an arena for mutual understanding. As I understand Gadamer, even before we begin consciously to reflect, our history has "effected"[6] or shaped in us pre-understandings which bias our thinking in this direction and not that. Gadamer speaks of this directionality as a prejudice—but Gadamer views prejudices not as inherently negative but inevitable and productive, the "biases of our openness to the world." We can't think outside of prejudices: we think through them.[7]

This does not mean, however, that we remain locked into our prejudices. Our prejudices generate the horizon of our current understandings: This is as far as I can see based on my current prejudices. Yet I can test my prejudices against yours. I can learn from you what horizon of understanding is available to you as a result of your prejudices. To the extent we can then mutually learn from sharing and testing our own prejudices against the other's, we experience a "fusion of horizons."[8] To put it too simply, we come to understand each other. Through that act of understanding, we enlarge our initial horizons. Now we can see farther than we could at the outset. Thus, as I explain below, prejudices, rather than simply being bad things to grow out of, can be treasures through which we help each other gain ever expanding horizons.

Now much of Gadamer's thought focuses on how we understand texts rather than other people. Thus in appropriating Gadamer as I do in this chapter, I may stretch his thought beyond its own primary prejudices.[9] Hopefully, however, this is not simply a violation of Gadamer but an example of what happens when another horizon fuses with his.

Having said that, let me move toward a more autobiographical treatment of effective history, prejudices, and horizons than Gadamer might normally inspire but which my appropriation of Gadamer over the years has led me to value. Along with Frederick Buechner, who once memorably said that "most theology . . . is essentially autobiography,"[10] a statement I might extend to "all acts of understanding and communication are essentially autobiography," I conclude that one way we come to view our own and the other's prejudices as treasures is to see them in the context of our own and the other's life stories. My particular experience of effective history shapes these prejudices in given ways to yield given horizons. The same is true for you. Let me briefly tell my story. If we were face to face, it would then be your turn to tell your story.

AUTOBIOGRAPHICAL ROOTS OF THE JOURNEY

Along perhaps with most in my Baby Boomer generation, I had no idea when I was growing up that homosexuality would one day become an "issue" instead of an abomination. I grew up breathing what was in the mid-twentieth-century air (or effective history) and mostly had been for millennia: Homosexuals are perverts. There aren't many of them. You've probably never met one and you don't want to.

Until the 1970s, when a loved one told me she was lesbian. And a young woman I had known since childhood told me the same thing. Suddenly the air seemed to have shifted as dramatically as it does when a cold front blows out a warm front and within minutes temperatures tumble, clouds scud, and the very color and feel of the atmosphere is so transformed reality itself seems altered.

From many quadrants came confirmation of this shift, as in that same year suddenly homosexuality as an issue to battle over erupted at Eastern Mennonite, the college I was attending. Now not only the prejudice that homosexuality is bad was shaping horizons of understanding; more radically than ever before the prejudice that homosexuality can be good was emerging. Horizons were suddenly in dramatic flux.

I had started attending EMC in 1972. The 1960s were over, but 1972's graduating class had been first-year students in 1968. They had arrived on campus during that explosive, historic, and climactic year of the decade in which riots, assassinations, worsening conditions in Vietnam, beatings at the Democratic convention, and public lovemaking in make-love-not-war mode seemed to mark the end of the established order, whether cultural, economic, political, or moral.

Not only did I imbibe the whiff of revolution still clinging to many students on campus who had gone to school with the class of 1972, I also brought to campus my own rebellions against my near-fundamentalist Mennonite missionary kid background. Until earlier that year, I had been raised largely in Cuba and Mexico in the set-apart world of Mennonite missionaries who had often arrived on the mission field in the plain, Amish-like clothing many Mennonites wore in those days. I had been thoroughly socialized within the effective history of a people who for centuries had lived outside the mainstream and whose prejudices were that the mainstream was "the world" and we God's true people.

What my parents' generation didn't quite grasp until too late was that books could open a doorway out of any enclave. Through books I entered that odd, wonderful, mad world of mainstream, often secular culture, and began to find its prejudices as compelling as those my upbringing had inculcated in me. Through books I entered a world in which even the existence of God seemed unprovable. So, no doubt partly as a grand adolescent nose-thumbing, I decided early in my teens that this missionary kid would be a secular atheist, his horizons of understanding so much vaster than those of theists.

Although by the time I entered college the atheism had mellowed somewhat into agnosticism, and a wistful one at that (I wanted to believe but wasn't sure how), my bias was toward the margins—of belief, church, culture. As I blended that prejudice with influence of students still exuding the 1960s, I came to fancy myself something of a radical. And when a radical began to learn that friends and family members were gay or lesbian, he was willing to leap quickly, after the first shock, toward seeing them as unjustly marginalized.

Then for a few years, at least in my own life, the issue seemed to go into hibernation. I went to seminary, graduated, and was called to my first pastorate, at Germantown Mennonite Church in Philadelphia. The oldest Mennonite congregation in North America, Germantown had been founded in 1683 by Mennonite and Quaker families. Its fortunes had ebbed and flowed over the years, until in 1982, when I was hired, the congregation was down to about twenty-five participants and had not had a paid pastor in years.

Among those participating were some of conservative mindset who doubted, possibly rightly, the wisdom of hiring this radical fresh out of seminary. By this time I was a Christian. I had been helped a few years before by Pascal's wager (better to try faith and be wrong than not to try it and be wrong, as I summarized it) and in college and seminary by growing awareness that it was more possible than I had once understood to engage hard questions while on a journey toward faith. I had come to see that not only theism but also atheism and secularism were prejudices and to conclude that I wanted to learn from all these prejudices rather than remain locked in the limited horizons of any. I also remained drawn to the margins and saw the Jesus who proclaimed release to captives, healed lepers, and turned despised Samaritans into heroes as himself a minister to the marginalized.

When during my first year at Germantown a gay man began to attend, I sent signals from the pulpit that here there was welcome. By this time the congregation was growing quickly as other Mennonites who had sought exile in the city from conservative rural backgrounds found at Germantown a haven and began, in turn, to marginalize those original more conservative attenders. So I was not alone in welcoming the gay participant. Nor was I alone in seeing offering welcome as the righteous path and those opposing welcome as risking opposition to Christ. We knew our prejudice, and we knew it as the right one.

We and I were sincere, I believe, in that welcome, and it took us far. It spurred our adopting as the congregation's position that, amid the controversies over what Scripture says about homosexuality, we preferred to risk erring on the side of grace rather than judgment.

At the same time, how tempted we humans are, in our frailties and fallenness, to mix motives. How then to know what proportion of motive was purehearted welcome and what proportion the sheer exhilaration of feeling righteous against villainous opposition?

This was a question I at least began to struggle with as our congregational stand took us internally into marginalizing the dissenters among us and externally into head-on collision with the regional Mennonite denominational body to which we belonged, a collision perhaps made inevitable by the national visibility the congregation's historic status afforded. Part of me wanted to make a heroic stand even at the expense of excommunication. Yet gradually I came to believe that the part of me committed to extending a welcome I could trust. I truly did sense a call from Scripture, the model of Jesus, and even, I hope, the Holy Spirit, to welcome all. But the part of me tempted to use extending a welcome to position myself as the righteous one battling the unrighteous, some of whom I was even pastoring, was less trustworthy.

My conclusion that it was less trustworthy was nurtured by the fact that I was already drawn to a kind of rudimentary anticipation of the Gadamerian theory I would later find so fruitful. I was drawn to the growing conviction that any perspective has treasure to offer. Therefore it would be simplistic to believe that if Germantown and I entered battle with our denomination, our side would be the only righteous one. I had already been through one searing round of being shaped by, then rejecting, then finding fresh ways to be enriched by the prejudices of my fundamentalist theistic background even as I learned from agnostic and secularist prejudices. I would need to find a different path than simply to lead a heroic resistance movement against Satan's minions. I would need to find a path that honored both a horizon of understanding shaped by prejudice toward welcome and a horizon enlarged by the prejudice of the majority that an unnuanced welcome was too simple a treatment of homosexuality.

ALTERNATIVES TO BATTLE

Thus began my quest for an alternative to battle. It led toward my supporting congregational discussions with our denominational body in search of a way to continue welcoming all—yet not in a spirit of directly confronting the denominational position that full sexual intimacy and bonding is reserved for a man and a woman.

Gradually this led to an uneasy truce. One level of the truce was within me. I had moved so quickly from shock to welcome when I first learned of friends and loved ones who were lesbian or gay that I had not fully engaged the full range of my own questions. Now I took more time to ponder the teachings within which I had been raised and to wonder to what extent they still deserved consideration even after being subjected to critical evaluation. I didn't find myself fully swayed back to the understandings I had earlier unthinkingly held. In fact it does seem to me careful exegesis both of Bible and culture leads to more complexities in this area than we once were aware of. Does the Bible truly speak to to the full range of our current understandings of sexuality? Is it really tenable to claim to be able to hate the "sin" but love the "sinner"? And if not tenable, then what is the church's responsibility for the horrors perpetrated by homophobes?

On the other hand, are any of us, individually as well as communally, churches as well as cultures, wise enough to be sure we're getting our exegesis of Bible or culture right when in one generation we reject many thought-to-be-settled prejudices regarding how we should view homosexuality? Are we wise enough to know what negative as well as positive consequences may flow from overturning in the blink of an eye the heterocentrist views of sexuality the effective histories of culture and church led us to consider beyond discussion within many of our lifetimes?

For me personally the truce involved a commitment to think and act more slowly than I had until then. I needed to learn to value the gems of insight in a range of prejudices, not merely to leap to quick judgment that I already knew all truth and now simply must do what I could to impose it on others.

Even at the personal level, such a truce was tenuous. Much more tenuous was the truce reached at the congregational level: As long as we didn't formally take a position opposing denominational teachings, our denominational body would give the congregation some space to discern on a case-by-case basis the shape of welcome. In practice this tended to mean that we would consider formally welcoming into membership gay or lesbian participants willing to acknowledge the "potential brokenness" of their situation and actions.

This was certainly no perfect outcome. It seemed too lax to some. To others it was simply a new vocabulary of marginalization: "You're saying you'll welcome us—but only if we agree to continue to see our gay or lesbian affections as conceivably sinful rather than as just as much a gift in God's eyes as your heterosexuality." But it survived my remaining years as pastor at Germantown.

Then in 1989 I became a book editor and watched Germantown developments from afar. In 1992 I entered a Ph.D. program in rhetoric and communication at Temple University. By 1995, as I continued my studies, it became ever clearer that any truce between Germantown and Franconia Conference, the denominational body to which Germantown was most immediately accountable, was breaking down. For two years an intense process of delegate deliberations unfolded. Finally in 1997 a five-to-one majority voted to excommunicate Germantown.

During those years I was seeking the right dissertation topic. I proposed an ambitious theorizing, using Michel Foucault and Gadamer, of American cultural wars. My wiser-than-I adviser vetoed me. I tried for a much smaller project based on receiving survey responses from pastors. Of over 200 approached, a handful responded. Not workable. Then where, asked my adviser, might there already be in motion a conflict I could study? I pointed to the Germantown-Franconia conflict but stressed I didn't want to study that. Too close to home. My adviser vetoed me again.

APPLYING GADAMER TO PRODUCE *FRACTURED DANCE*

So eighty pages of transcribed discussions at three different delegate cluster sessions became my dissertation research database. And the philosophical hermeneutics of Gadamer provided the theory for interpreting the data. Through Gadamer, I looked for ways to create markers of Gadamerian or "genuine" conversation and assess their presence or absence in the Germantown-Franconia deliberations.

The complexities of that quest are recorded in the book based on the dissertation, *Fractured Dance: Gadamer and a Mennonite Conversation on Homosexuality*, so I will not try to reiterate them here. Rather, let me note that, as foreshadowed in the preceding pages of this chapter, after years of wrestling with Gadamer at the level of both theory and application, and surely at great risk of oversimplification, I have come to summarize genuine conversation as involving a mutual quest for treasure in our own and the other's viewpoint. This entails making two key moves. The first move is "to make as clear as I can why I hold this position [prejudice] and why you might find in it treasure to value in your own quest for truth." The second key move is "to see the value in the other's view [prejudice] and to grow in my own understandings by incorporating as much of the other's perspective as I can without losing the integrity of my own convictions."[11]

Such moves, underneath the ambiguities and complexities of theory, were at heart what I looked for in those eighty pages of delegate deliberations. As I reported in *Fractured Dance*,[12] I mostly didn't find them. I mostly witnessed that age-old dy-

154 / MUTUAL TREASURE

namic amid controversy: battle. The rhetoric revolved primarily around right-wrong: This is why I'm right; this is why you're wrong. These are the bad things that will happen if we do it your way.

That forced me to ask, in the more theoretical portions of *Fractured Dance*, whether the problem was with the delegates or my/Gadamer's theory. If the problem was with the delegates, then there it was—the possibility of genuine conversation—but they had fled it. If the problem was with the theory, then perhaps I was expecting the impossible. Perhaps I was using Gadamer to prescribe norms for conversation unlikely to be enacted by actual humans. Maybe this was a flaw in Gadamer—normative expectations imposed on the process of understanding rather than descriptive categories teased not out of the ways we wish humans would communicate but the ways we actually do.[13]

My conclusion then and now is this: Probably there is a flawed idealism both in Gadamer and my appropriation of his thought. Probably humans will mostly not see issues like homosexuality as arenas for mutual understanding instead of battle.

LOVING ENEMY PREJUDICES

But perhaps quixotically, I have felt impelled to continue the quest. One key reason for this, and a reason I was drawn to Gadamer in the first place, is that I was raised in a historic peace church tradition.[14] I was taught to love enemies. I was taught especially to love real enemies, literal enemies, enemies your nation considers so bad it wants to send you to kill them. I was taught that this is what Jesus taught, in the Sermon on the Mount. "You have heard that was said. . . . But I say to you. . . ." So my forebears were imprisoned by Woodrow Wilson's government rather than fighting in World War I. As conscientious objectors they did alternative service for FDR's and Harry Truman's governments rather than fight in World War II or Korea. And in the early 1970s, I registered as a CO in preparation not to go to Vietnam. But then the draft ended just after my name was assigned a lottery number, so I never had to find out what next.

While pursuing my graduate studies in communication even as my former congregation faced the rising odds of excommunication by brothers and sisters in Christ, it seemed a voice, small and still yet ever more insistent, whispered that maybe if Jesus taught us to love rather than kill human enemies, he would want us to love rather than kill our prejudice or viewpoint "enemies." And how do you love an enemy viewpoint without somehow learning from it, or at least respecting it, at least looking for nuggets of treasure in it even if you in the end persist in seeing much greater treasure in your own stand?

So *Fractured Dance* became my report on how communication turned out not to look like I wish it had. But it also remained one roadmap for what might yet someday be, if viewpoint enemies could be enticed into testing friendship, into testing the effects of treating an enemy prejudice as something not only to reject but also to try to love. In 2001, four years after Germantown was excommunicated, the book was published. There I mostly let the matter rest. Let its occasional readers do with the roadmap what they would.

APPLYING GADAMER TO PRODUCE
DREAMSEEKER MAGAZINE WINTER 2006

Then came 2006. Weldon Nisly, pastor of Seattle Mennonite Church, decided God had called him to officiate at a same-sex ceremony. The denominational body to which he was accountable eventually suspended his credentials.[15] Our primary denominational publication ran an editorial celebrating that after years of struggling with what to do in such situations, the denomination was now finding clarity and was able rather routinely to take effective action when positions on homosexuality at variance with denominational teachings emerged.

When it appeared that this would be the main treatment of Nisly's action in the denominational press, I was troubled. This seemed another step backward from learning to treat different viewpoints not as triggers for battle but as treasures for mutual learning. So I thought how interesting and perhaps redemptive it would be if not only Nisly but also the denominational officials who had decided to suspend his credentials wrote blood-sweat-and tears narratives of how they came to their respective positions and actions. The hope would be to move behind their public conflicts to the "take this cup from me" wrestlings likely all had experienced, regardless of their eventual conclusions.

Nisly soon agreed. But all denominational officials declined, noting their fear—possibly well-founded—that any public comment would only contribute to hurt rather than healing. I didn't want to publish Nisly in isolation; that risked perpetuating one prejudice against others, rather than bringing them into contact that might lead to mutual learning. So though giving up on publishing views of the specific leaders who had worked with Nisly's case, I looked for other writers, representing as many prejudices as possible, who could be published in a special issue of *DreamSeeker Magazine*.

The results were both exciting and disappointing. Exciting because to my knowledge *Dreamseeker Magazine* Winter 2006 represented one of the first times a Mennonite-related publication specifically aimed to view homosexuality as an arena for mutual learning rather than right-wrong battle. And the special issue, which was available free online,[16] circulated widely, hopefully disseminating a fresh approach.

But disappointing because even the special issue itself fell far short of my own dreams. Though strongly encouraged to show evidence of learning from viewpoints with which they disagreed, its writers tended to persist in seeing each other as combatants rather than partners in a quest for understandings larger than any alone could find.

And disappointing because it quickly became evident that the very act of putting together this special issue had itself fed conflictual energies. For instance, some were concerned (rightly, no doubt) that despite the stated goal of genuine conversation, the effect seemed to be to favor those who wanted to change the church's teachings, hence positioning the magazine on one side of ongoing combat rather than as an alternative to combat. Others were concerned (understandably) that all the writers were straight people talking about rather than being able to speak out of the community of gays or lesbians.

APPLYING GADAMER TO PRODUCE *STUMBLING TOWARD A GENUINE CONVERSATION ON HOMOSEXUALITY*

On the other hand, even in such disappointments seemed to be the seeds of a next step. If this was an effort at genuine conversation rather than combat, then fallibilities of one effort and the criticisms rightly highlighting them should be treated not as occasions for battle but opportunities to keep pursuing conversation. Thus, as I had hoped might happen even while working on Winter 2006, it became evident that the special issue was generating enough energy and feedback, both affirming and critical, to expand the conversation into a book.

So was born *Stumbling Toward a Genuine Conversation on Homosexuality*. Here the Winter 2006 articles became Part I of the larger work, and a twice-as-long Part II incorporated responses to Part One as well as extended the conversation in fresh directions and with new participants. Part Two featured positions probably sometimes more hard-hitting than in Part One and included more diverse conversation partners, from those who had long aimed to uphold the denomination's teachings, including several denominational leaders, to the gays and lesbians the teachings had marginalized or even ostracized.

Here again the effects were both exciting and disappointing. Exciting because now an even more substantive conversation aimed at mutual learning rather than combat had emerged. Exciting because, as one denominational leader noted in the book, "These voices are real. All of them are part of us. And that is why we need to listen to each other. To truly find where God is leading us as a church."[17] What an alternative to battle.

But disappointing because, as ever, the dominant moves probably remained those emerging from or at least congruent with battle: Why does it make more sense for me to hold this prejudice or position than yours? Why wouldn't you want to move then toward mine? And disappointing because, as several writers mentioned,[18] there is only so far toward "conversation" a set of chapters as opposed to persons conversing face-to-face can go. Published conversations tend to be static, side-by-side statements, whereas face-to-face conversations (or even e-mail, instant messages, and blogs) allow for a more dynamic give-and-take.

On the other hand, even amid the mixed record of the published conversations are hopeful hints. As one denominational leader who wished for face-to-face conversation noted, one reason it may have to begin in places like books is that other safe places for conversation are often not available.[19] Possibly, then, published conversations can enable conversations not unfolding elsewhere—or at least provide some of the soil from which safe spaces for other forms of conversation may eventually spring forth.

In addition, even as published conversations tend to be static, precisely their slower pace and lack of urgent need for reply may help writers think through to what extent they are able to see treasure in opposing prejudices. In *Stumbling*, for instance, many chapter authors who accepted the invitation to respond to the rest of the book showed evidence of seeking treasure even in what they mostly oppose. One striking example, of the many which could be offered, is provided by Harold Miller. He explains why he remains a conservative who has not changed his mind on homosexuality.[20] Yet later, noting aspects of the book that struck him, he highlights "Luke Miller's poetic prose on the Mennonite voices inside his head"[21]—even though Luke Miller is a gay author with whose conclusions Harold Miller would not agree.

Now out there *Stumbling* is, stumbling around. I doubt it will greatly change the world or Christian deliberations or even Mennonite conversations on homosexuality. It remains unclear to me whether humans, in general or Christian, are capable of sustained "genuine" conversation as opposed to seeing life as made up of binaries, one of which we champion, the other of which we aim to defeat. Homosexuality: Bad/Good. Right/Wrong. Forbidden in Scripture/Allowed or Even Celebrated by Scripture Properly Interpreted. Curse/Gift. All Nature/All Nurture. Changeable/Immutable. God Wants Welcome/God Wants Excommunication.

After spending decades now pursuing alternatives to battling over homosexuality, I see no overwhelming evidence that such a vision will carry the day. Nor am I even sure what carrying the day would look like. Would it mean a formal change in denomational teachings on homosexuality? A shift in polity so as to free regional bodies or local congregations to take positions of "faithful dissent" in relation to denominational stands? How would any denomination, Mennonite or otherwise, simultaneously affirm loving enemy viewpoints and maintain a modicum of clarity regarding denominational identity and teachings? There are many devils in such details I don't pretend to be wise enough to address. I suspect working them through them will be a task of many, within and across denominations, for generations to come. But then perhaps I need to break also out of the binary Carry the Day/Not Carry the Day. Even those writers whose chapters combined to form this book will disagree over what it means to love enemies. My historic peace church prejudice is a minority one. Does that mean it's wrong and the majority prejudices are right? Or is this the seed God has called a few of us to plant in the world, wherever and however it may take root—even as other writers in this book plant other seeds?

Maybe my job, our job, is not mainly to win, even when the quest is to stop dividing the world into Winners/Losers, My Prejudice Good/Your Prejudice Bad. Maybe our job is to plant, and God's job is to harvest. But whatever God harvests, I hope over time it will lead to fewer enemies and more brothers and sisters.

NOTES

1. Michael A. King, *Fractured Dance: Gadamer and a Genuine Conflict Over Homosexuality* (Telford, Pa.: Pandora Press U.S., 2001).

2. *DreamSeeker Magazine* 6.1 (Winter 2008).

3. Michael A. King, ed. *Stumbling Toward a Genuine Conversation on Homosexuality* (Telford, Pa.: Cascadia Publishing House, 2007).

4. Hans-Georg Gadamer, *Philosophical Hermeneutics*, trans. and ed. David E. Linge (Berkeley: University of California, 1976), p. 9.

5. Hans-Georg-Gadamer, *Truth and Method*, 2nd. rev. ed., trans. Joel Weinsheimer and Donald G. Marshall (New York: Continuum, 1994; original work pub. 1960), p. 306.

6. Gadamer, *Truth and Method*, pp. 301-302

7. Gadamer, *Philosophical Hermeneutics*, p. 9; see also *Truth and Method*, pp. 269-277.

8. Gadamer, *Truth and Method*, pp. 306-307.

9. I comment on these issues in considerable detail in *Fractured Dance*, ch. 5, especially pp. 155-171.

10. Frederick Buechner, *The Alphabet of Grace* (New York: Crossroad Books, 1970), p. 3.

11. *Stumbling Toward a Genuine Conversation on Homesexuality*, p. 26.

12. *Fractured Dance*, chs. 4, 7.

13. See *Fractured Dance*, particularly chapter 5, for a detailed look at such considerations.

14. This is fleshed out in *Stumbling Toward a Genuine Conversation on Homosexuality*, pp. 116-119.

15. Weldon Nisly, " To Guide Our Feet," in *Stumbling Toward a Genuine Conversation on Homosexuality*, pp. 42-48.

16. www.CascadiaPublishingHouse.com/dsm/winter06/current. htm.

17. J. Ron Byler, "The Last Word," in *Stumbling Toward a Genuine Conversation on Homosexuality*, p. 310.

18. Carolyn Schrock-Shenk, "Foreword"; Jeanine Czubaroff, "Afterword"; Byler, "The Last Word"; in *Stumbling Toward a Genuine Conversation on Homosexuality*, pp. 16, 304-307, 309.

19. Byler, "The Last Word," p. 310.

20. Harold N. Miller, "A Conservative Who Could Change on Homosexuality—But So Far Has Not," in *Stumbling Toward a Genuine Conversation on Homosexuality*, pp. 149-163

21. Harold N. Miller, "Stumbling Forward: Some Impressions," in *Stumbling Toward a Genuine Conversation on Homosexuality*, p. 287.

Chapter 9

Finding Light in Broken Hope: An Alternative to Adversarial Criminal Justice

Tammy Krause[1]

Tammy Krause did her undergraduate studies at Gonzaga University (Spokane, Wash.). She holds a masters degree in Conflict Transformation from Eastern Mennonite University (Harrisonburg, Va.). Krause began doctoral studies in law in 2007 at the University of Manchester, England. She is a member of All Saints Episcopal Church in Phoenix, Arizona, although she currently attends St. Clement's Church of England in Chorlton cum Hardy, Manchester, UK.

Before the work on which she reports in this essay, Krause worked for ten years in the field of conflict transformation. Her initiatives included being a part of the Christian Peacemaker Teams, a volunteer with Sojourners in Washington, D. C., and a volunteer with Brethren Volunteer Service.

Since 1997, Krause has pioneered a program called *Defense-Initiated Victim Outreach,* working on federal capital cases throughout the United States. She works on behalf of the defense teams representing the accused in groundbreaking cases, creating professional relationships with the victim's family in an effort to bridge the historical gap between the two sides. Krause's work awarded her two fellowships, a Soros Justice Fellowship (1998-2000) and an Askoka:

Innovators for the Public Fellowship (2001-2004). She worked for the Federal Public Defender in 2003-2007, assisting defense teams nationwide, training individuals in the defense-initiated victim outreach model she created, and speaking nationally about the work. She has been a faculty member at the Summer Peacemaking Institute at Eastern Mennonite University and has led legal trainings at the Boalt School of Law and the Washington & Lee School of Law.

Emily Dickinson speaks of hope as "the thing with feathers / That perches in the soul, / And sings the tune without the words. . . ." Deep within us lies the redemptive value of hope. This is a foundational belief of mine that I must share with you. Hope is not something to be portrayed as insubstantial—the thing with feathers—or to be quietly dismissed—and sings the tune without the words—because it is the essence of these images that embody the power of faith. Faith often is not something that can be put into words but must be understood through experience. As a Christian, I have found it important to be able to express my faith in practical ways. How can one hold onto the mystery of faith if there are no handlebars, so to speak?

It was in my hunger to search for God in the everyday that I came to know the truth that hope provides in our faith journey. Quakers speak of the "light of God" that is within every person; in essence, each of us has a spark of God dwelling in us. The belief that God resides in everyone and is a stranger to no one led me toward a vocation where few see light, let alone promise. But I believe that hope is nestled in the core of that light, for I have seen it. This is my attempt to put it into words for you.

BROKEN HOPE

Leslie Mazzara and Adriane Insogna were two vibrant women who had their lives ahead of them. As anyone could imagine for women in their mid-twenties, life seemed full of promise in work, friendships, and possibility. On the night of October 31, 2004, after Adriane, Leslie, and another roommate, Lauren Meanza, passed out Halloween candy to children, they turned in for the night. Hours later, an intruder broke into their home, went upstairs, and violently killed Leslie and Adriane, while Lauren was able to escape.

The horror of this crime bore many injustices and indignities for their families. The media was incessant in covering the crime, with headlines screaming, "Nightmare in the Wine Country," "Halloween Massacre," "Beauty Queen Killed." Despite the private horror for the families and the public fear for the community, the media focused on the crime because both women were well-loved, educated, and beautiful—not your "typical" victims.

Family members, current boyfriends, and former boyfriends from afar were subjected to police scrutiny and requests for DNA while Eric Copple, the person who committed the crime, went about his life, marrying his childhood girlfriend and joining her while she was interviewed by a major network about Leslie's and Adriane's death. At one point, Lily Prudhomme, Adriane's best friend and Copple's wife said, "Somebody must know something. Somebody would have had to notice their friend acting strange or having bruises. Doesn't seem like someone could walk away from it acting fine."[2] It appeared that speculation affected by youth and beauty influenced both the police and the media's perception of what transpired in Adriane and Leslie's deaths.

But what happens to families when their loved ones are murdered? Where is their right to preserve the memory of their loved one the way they see best? When did it become the media's right to violate the private lives of women who were simply sleeping in their own beds when they were killed? How are the families able to grieve their loss privately when the media pays little attention to how the news headlines deepen the family's pain? And turning toward the judicial system, how are families notified of the death of their loved one? How does the death of a family member give the government the right to consider itself the victim of the crime? What rights do family members have to voice their concern about the judicial proceedings against the accused? How can families feel a sense of justice and dignity both for them and their loved one?

THE LEGAL FACES FAMILIES MEET

It is in the tide of these questions that I find myself listening, thinking, and working to find answers that are acceptable to families who have lost their loved ones to murder.[3] My role is neither as a counselor or a pastor but, rather, on behalf of the accused. I work in a profession called *defense-initiated victim outreach* and work with defense attorneys who represent men and women charged with a capital offense. My job is to reach out to the victim's family and to develop a professional relationship with them throughout the judicial process. This is an unlikely position, given the contrariety of the defense team's responsibility of defending its client. It is also work met with great suspicion due to the politicization of the role of the victim and at the same time the castigation of the victim within the judicial system. Yet it is precisely because of this tension that outreach to families is so vital for both the victim and the accused. I believe that any time a group or individuals have a prescribed role and in carrying out that role are summarily silenced in regard to the procession of justice (whether as the victim or the accused), then the legal system has created a vacuum of power that only serves itself.

While many legal professionals advocate for victims, it is usually for their own professional benefit. Both sides of the legal fence view victims as an entity that needs to be controlled throughout the duration of the case to ensure their side's strategy wins. This is often due to the adversarial nature of the legal system in which one side must always have something "over" the other side with which to win a case. Because victims garner public sympathy and have become a political issue in recent decades, it is strategic to have the victim supporting your legal platform. Who wants to be viewed in the public eye as ignoring the interests of the victim? One of the many tasks for the legal teams is to appear to stand for what is honorably/decently right and for what the victims support, whether that is the right to a fair trial or the belief in retribution.[4]

Prosecuting attorneys state in front of the jury or in the media, "The victim deserves justice," or "We have listened to the victims and are moving forward with the case because of their support." State and local prosecutors hold elected positions and often run campaigns extolling a "pro-victim" platform which is not about being "tough on crime" but rather tough on criminals. While the prosecution may zealously pursue an accused person, what is the actual benefit to the victim?

On the other hand, defense attorneys have been known to question the relevance of victims of the crime in the case against their client. Defense attorneys commonly work to strike or limit a victim's testimony, arguing that such testimony would be detrimental by biasing the jury's opinion of what should happen to their client. It has also been argued that defense attorneys intimidate and even bully victims in the courtroom and on the witness stand.

As one can imagine, it would be difficult to be a victim of a crime under any circumstance, but to have to face an adversarial system whose tentacles can re-injure the person harmed is a challenge. It is understandable that such an environment can be daunting and undesirable to any person being forced to participate in it. It is common for victims not to appear in court or choose not to engage the legal system as a coping mechanism and out of self-protection.

For ten years I have worked with families who have been forced into the judicial system due to extremely unfortunate circumstances. Defense attorneys who had grown weary of ignoring victims yet did not know how to approach family members of the deceased or how it would impact the work on behalf of their client were the impetus for work that would come to be called defense-initiated victim outreach.[5] This work stems from the concern of the Restorative Justice movement to create more balance among the parties impacted by the crime and to address their needs in a judicial context.[6]

The request from this group of attorneys to think differently about how to work with victims and surviving family members during the pre-trial and trial process could be viewed skeptically. One could make cynical assumptions about the defense attorneys' motivations. But because I am one of the people who was asked to work with the attorneys, to create this dialogue between two unseemingly sides and forge a new field of work, I can verify that while never losing sight of clients, their motives were noble and brave.[7] It was these qualities that ignited that spark of hope in me to walk into a new field of work that attempts to create a balance between the needs and rights of the victim and the accused.

Coming Alongside Families

Cathy Harrington, a Unitarian Universalist minister, is Leslie Mazzara's mother. In the months following Leslie's death, Cathy struggled to find her voice in many arenas—in her church, in her relationship with God, in her beliefs, and in the legal case against Eric Copple. Not one to sit idle, Cathy sought advice on how to be more included in the judicial process. Through people who knew that there was a different approach to working within the adversarial system, I was put in contact with Cathy and shortly thereafter with Arlene Allen, Adriane Insogna's mother. After several phone conversations and e-mails, we agreed to meet in person to discuss the possibility of seeking a more active voice for the two families in the case.

On a September afternoon, several family members from both women's families and I met for the first time at a restaurant in Napa, California. We sat around a large table as we politely and awkwardly ordered lunch while we waited for the "real" conversation, the one about how and why I could help the families in the case against Copple, to begin. As most first meetings with victims' families go, I was questioned about my family life, upbringing, political views, faith, hobbies, education, work, and especially my role in working on behalf of defense attorneys.

I spent the majority of the lunch meeting answering the families' questions and listening to their skepticism and concerns. At times such as this, it is important to listen to the apprehension without an answer or argument. People need to be heard and to feel valued for what they have to say—this is common sense but we forget this in an adversarial system. We think that we must have a counterpoint for each point that is made; otherwise we might lose our standing. This is where I believe the law has lost some good judgment. The deepest longing in humanity is for connection. Part of what creates connection is listening and validation, and it is often because legal professionals are so concerned with credibility rather than connection that we miss the very thing we are striving for. It surprises me how often I get asked by legal professionals, "You answer their questions honestly?" to which I reply, "How could I not?"

It is important to live with integrity and to know that I engage people with honesty and care. What is more, families are already in a horrible situation to which I do not want to add further harm. While these are personal reasons for being candid with family members, there are several professional reasons for it as well. Victims have very little choice in the judicial arena and because of this; they will exercise what options they do have with a good deal of discernment. Also, because defense-initiated victim outreach is a relatively new legal approach, it is uncommon for victims to know about it or to be fully informed about the values and the praxis, which adds to their scrutiny.

One thing I have learned about families who have lost a loved one to murder is this: They gain an acute ability to know when someone is telling the truth and can be trusted. If one does not pass muster in the initial conversation (I have seen this happen), it is unlikely that a family will continue productive engagement. But most importantly, if we are asking family members to be in a professional relationship with us, one different from what the adversarial model offers, we have to be models for what is possible within the law. My question to those in the broader community is this: If we do not engage with victims in new ways, why should we expect them to choose the different approach we advocate?

NOT TO BE DISMISSED

The Insogna and Allen and the Mazzara and Harrington families did not have great demands of the judicial process. They were families torn by the murders. There was not full agreement as to whether to push for a trial, to support the government seeking the death penalty against Copple, or many other factors that go into a capital case. Where there was consensus was that the families wanted to avoid having their daughter's, sister's, and nieces' lives questioned and their deaths to be the memory that remained.

A part of my job is to discover what family members need from the legal system. Often, when one is amid a crisis or affected by trauma, it is difficult to have clarity not only about *what* one needs but *how* to go about meeting those needs. Because I am not directly impacted by the devastating loss and am experienced with how the legal system works, I listen to family members with the approach of naming what I hear being said and asking if it is important to the family. In listening to and working with the families over the course of a couple of months, I compiled a list of judicial possibilities that could address the families' various interests.

When I met with Adriene's and Leslie's families to share what I had heard them name as important, they were surprised that they did know what they needed from the legal system. They were concerned about Copple making any profit from his life or the deaths of Adriane and Leslie since the case had captured press attention. The families also were concerned about the details of the women's deaths becoming more fodder for the media and wanted to avoid the information being released publically. There were other issues, but the overriding concern was that the families were tired of any focus or attention on Copple and wanted to separate him from Leslie and Adriane. After discussing such concerns, the families decided that they wanted to pursue having these issues formally addressed by Copple and by the government.

A group of family members met with the district attorney and the lead prosecuting attorney on the Copple case and explained to the attorneys that although they would support the government in its pursuit of going to trial and seeking the death penalty, they wanted to see if the government would be willing to negotiate a plea agreement with Eric Copple through the defense team based on the list of concerns compiled by the families. The families told the attorneys that they did not want to have a trial for which someone had already admitted to the crime or through which the media would be able to exploit the details discussed in court. Although the government was not prepared for this type of dialogue with the families, the conversation was productive and hopeful. The families gave their list of judicial interests to the district attorney and waited for a response from the legal teams.[8]

FEELING ONE'S WINGS

One of the most anxious moments in work such as this is having to tell families there are no guarantees their concerns will be recognized, addressed, or agreed to by either the attorneys (for both sides) or the accused. Victims place hope in a system—and a person whose actions were the antithesis of hope—whose very nature extracts optimism from its core.[9] But hope is a mysterious thing—it continues to rise despite our experiences and shows us what is possible. The challenge is to find a balance between waiting for the possible and preparing for the alternative. How does the spirit allow for hope when another person's actions destroyed one's very evidence of it?

This is a question of mystery and one that only those who have experienced it can answer fully. Since I am not a person in that situation and have only witnessed such courageous acts, my answer is a mixture of speculation. When I work on a case, I do what I can to help move it in a positive direction. With hard work, perseverance, and intelligence I can help legal teams and victims understand the options available as a possible resolution to a case with potential to be agreeable to all parties. While these attributes may be persuasive for attorneys, I believe such qualities alone would not be enough for most family members. As mentioned earlier, I believe that connection to others is essential and over time builds trust and nurtures hope that an alternative may be possible. Most families are not familiar with the judicial system and are surprised by the hardened attitudes and inflexibility of legal professionals—starting with the police who inform them of their loved one's death to the attorneys' behavior. In time, mistrust becomes a learned behavior for families as well, as they see that there is no place for humanity in a courtroom. Yet when legal professionals do their job *and* make an effort to bridge the historical gap concerning the victims, cases often go places no one would have expected.

FINDING LIGHT

Two months after the families met with the Napa Valley district attorney's office to inquire about a potential plea agreement, Eric Copple accepted responsibility for his crimes and pleaded guilty in exchange for two life sentences and a list of conditions based on the families' concerns.[10] After the meeting with the families, the district attorney's office met with Copple's defense attorneys to advise them of the families' interests in precluding a trial if Copple were to accept responsibility for the crimes and other conditions. Both legal teams had to balance their responsibilities to the law, to their advocacy, and to the best interests of those who would be most impacted by the outcome. In the process, the two legal teams along with Mr. Copple were able to agree on a settlement that focuses on many of the families' judicial needs.

"I am pleased with the outcome. It is the best thing that could happen for all of the families involved. I don't want to spend the rest of my life worrying what Mr. Copple is doing," Arlene Allen said after the hearing.[11] A partial list of conditions that Copple agreed to includes these: to not talk with anyone other than legal or medical professionals about the crime, to not profit from the story of Adriane and Leslie's death, to end his right to appeal the conviction or sentence, and, with the guidance of a trained professional, to meet with any family members who wanted to talk with him.

A month later, the judge formally sentenced Eric Copple to life in prison. It is common for families for both the defendant and the victims to read a statement in court at this hearing. The defendant also has the right to make a statement if he or she chooses. Families and friends for both Leslie and Adriane gave powerful, emotional speeches of love and loss. In turn, Copple not only addressed the court but also turned and spoke to the families directly. "Arlene, Cathy, I am sorry for stealing your beloved Adriane and Leslie. Paul, Andy, Lexie, and Allison, I am so sorry for taking your precious sister from you," Copple sobbed.[12]

When court was adjourned, Cathy Harrington asked to be introduced to Eric Copple's mother. In the court foyer, conversations took place between families, defense attorneys, and the prosecution. The day's events would have seemed impossible a few months earlier: Copple accepted responsibility and apologized to the families, the judicial process against him was completely over, the grisly details of Leslie and Adriane's deaths were kept to a minimum in the public courtroom, and the judge limited the media's access to the people involved who requested it.

LISTENING TO A NEW TUNE OF AN OLD SONG

After the court session was over, the women's families and friends assembled for a private lunch. The mood was a mixture of relief, sadness, disbelief, and levity. Conversations flitted between funny and nostalgic memories of Adriane and Leslie and upcoming plans of trips, births, and moves. All were aware of the reason that they were there, yet in some ways, Copple was already becoming less prominent in their lives. At one point Arlene said, "It is hard to believe that we achieved a plea agreement. When we first sat down at that restaurant a few months ago, I didn't think that the attorneys would listen to us. I just didn't think we had any power."

It is these moments that make me continue with my work. The Insogna and Allen and Mazzara and Harrington families defied their sense of powerlessness and, with dignity, demanded to be valued in the judicial process. The odds that the families faced in having their interests considered, negotiated, and made conditional to a plea agreement were tremendous. The description of the work in the paragraphs above does not adequately describe the pressure that death penalty cases create nor does it detail all of the work, cooperation, and difficulties getting a plea agreement that both legal sides would accept. One has to remember that the government has the authority to take legal action against the accused and the defense team's job is to protect and deny any responsibility for their client. Neither of these roles officially mandates recognition of or responsibility to the victims. Yet it was because the victims offered both legal sides compelling reasons to listen to their judicial concerns that the case moved to judicial finality.

When one steps back from the adversarial nature of the legal system, it seems right for the people who were harmed to have a more active role in the process. The work that was done on this case did not violate Eric Copple's constitutional rights and in fact saved him from the possibility of being executed. It spared the families years of involvement in the judicial system. As well as the impact such an agreement had on the victims and the offender, it also saved court time and tax dollars.

All of these reasons are concrete and significant, alone worthy of commendation. But these aspects do not speak to the essence of why victims seek an alternative to a trial against the accused. As a witness to families who choose this path, I have come to hold that it is the belief in humanity and decency that compels families to work with this approach, even when one is unable to see the light in the accused. Goodness may have been shattered but cannot be silenced—for it does sing when we cannot find the words and sometimes cannot even hear the song.

Leslie Mazzara and Adriane Insogna were two women looking forward to each new experience in their lives. The senselessness of their deaths disrupted the lives of many—causing unfathomable horror and crises for their family and friends as well as the larger community. Yet, despite this, and even more inexplicable, is the hope which rises in surviving family members that somehow the person who killed their loved one will acknowledge his actions and be remorseful. This hope is *not* about reconciliation with the offender but about the defendant's acceptance of responsibility to end the judicial process and to release the family from its suspension, allowing them to more fully grieve given that the legal case is finished. For families, this is the least the offender can do. Cathy Harrington, in her victim impact statement at Mr. Copple's sentencing hearing, expressed the mixture of emotions that come from such a time and place:

"I am told, Mr. Copple, that you have found God since your senseless rampage. Certainly while finding God sets you on the road to redemption, God does not grant cheap grace. . . . I know that I will navigate the rest of my life with a broken heart. As a mother and as a minister I wish that I could tell you that I forgive you. At this time, I cannot. In fact, I can imagine one day, when the shock and pain of hearing what Leslie endured eases, I might likely wish you were sitting on death row. Maybe it will make me feel better to know that you will spend the rest of your life sitting in prison wondering when and how you will die: waiting, wondering when they will come to kill you—terrified. It may only seem fair after what you have done.

"The German poet Rainer Marie Rilke suggests that we think of God as a direction. I do vow to walk in the direction of forgiveness toward God. Not for your sake but for my own. I may never get there, but I know if I do not try, anger and hatred will likely kill what is left of this broken body of mine. If I do not try, I will also make a mockery of Leslie's belief in life."[13]

Being present to the unfolding of a person's pain and struggle is an incredible gift. When persons grapple with disbelief in their capacity to move forward or their ability to find their voice and to witness person after person—including Eric Copple—

face the challenges within themselves and honor that truth, one gets a sense of what God meant by "do not be afraid for I am with you."[14]

Such moments do not happen often in my work. But I can tell you that when you journey alongside persons faithfully and witness their dark moments of pain and suffering, there will be a time that you will find yourself present as they find their voices, as they sing the song which never stops, and you know you are in a very holy place.

MAINTAINING ONE'S FLIGHT ON THE JOURNEY

Jesus did not ask us to take the easy road in our walk as people of faith. We were not promised comfortable seats with a great view. It is difficult to face the horror of another person's actions that resulted in terrible and untimely deaths. If we step back and recall what is asked of us, we are not told to fix things, to look busy, or to have all of the answers; we are merely asked to be faithful. I cannot say that I have always been grateful for this calling nor that I have always wanted to remain on this road. God and I have had many tumbles (and rumbles) as I have struggled with fear, anger, impotence, and my own ego. It is not easy to witness people in pain and not want to "do something."

The balance I have found that allows me to continue with this work is an inexact science. It is a combination of many skills and a bit of mystery. Without honesty, integrity, hard work, a willingness to be vulnerable, and letting go of one's ego, I do not think the work would be successful. Yet deeper than that and more difficult to explain is the agreement that God and I are on this walk together. Through mindfulness and a commitment to being a presence to people suffering tragic loss, I try to help ease their pain by working on just solutions that will enable them to focus on more important matters. Sometimes this seems very minor in the magnitude of all that a victim faces, and I wonder if more needs to be done. Then I remember the words of the Talmud that resonate in me, "You are not required to complete the task, yet you are not free to withdraw from it."[15] When my work on a case is complete, I send up a prayer of gratitude for experiencing holiness in such unexpected places and another for the light that hope brings.

NOTES

1. The author would like to thank the families of Leslie Mazzara and Adriane Insogna for their support in telling their story in this chapter. Without their incredible trust in me, this story would not be told as it is today. I am indebted to Cathy Harrington and Arlene Allen for their grace, strength and determination to make this world a better place. You are amazing mothers.

2. Lily Prudhomme was interviewed by CBS' *48 Hours* for a show that aired November 19. 2005, three weeks after Eric Copple, her husband, turned himself into the police for the murders of Leslie and Adriane. Prodhomme was interviewed in October 2005.

3. Writing or talking about my work always carries the risk that I too am perpetrating in the families' trauma. It is a difficult task to talk about the facts of the crime or the harms inflicted upon the families without violating the relationship I have with each family. It is important for people who work with victims of any circumstance to carefully assess their motives for discussing the work in a public forum.

4. For an interesting juxtaposition of this point, look at three *Washington Post* articles by Jerry Markon and Timothy Dwyer regarding the *US v. Moussaoui* trial, the man accused of being the twentieth hijacker of the 11 September 2001 attacks. The articles will show how both legal teams had victims and surviving victim family members support their position of justice. "At Moussaoui trial, recalling lives stolen by 9/11," 11 April 2006; "Pentagon attack recalled at trial, Moussaoui prosecutors shift to spotlight local terror on 9/11," 12 April 2006; "Moussaoui gets some unusual help, some 9/11 relatives testify for defense," 20 April 2006.

5. For more of an in-depth explanation of the work known as defense-initiated victim outreach, read Tammy Krause, "Reaching Out to the Other Side: Defense-Based Victim Outreach in Capital Cases," in *Wounds That Do Not Bind: Victim-Based Perspectives on the Death Penalty*, ed. James Acker and David Karp (Durham, N.C.: Carolina Academic Press, 2006), pp. 379-396.

6. To learn more about restorative justice, read the seminal book by Howard Zehr, *Changing Lenses* (Scottdale, Pa.: Herald Press, 1990).

7. It is an honor to continue to call Dick Burr, Tim McVeigh's attorney and visionary for this work, a mentor, colleague, and friend.

8. Gary Lieberstein and Mark Boessenecker, the Napa County district attorney and assistant district attorney, were exemplary counsel in working with an approach unfamiliar to them. Both men maintained balance and integrity in relation to the case and to their word with the families throughout the pretrial plea negotiations and sentencing of Eric Copple.

9. This is true, unless you choose to believe in the legal arguments and remedies of television shows such as *Boston Legal* or *Law & Order*.

10. This plea agreement could not have happened without the dedication and work of Eric Copple's defense attorneys, Greg Galeste and Amy Morton. These attorneys worked hard to understand the importance of the families' concerns and to convey these to Mr. Copple in order to come to an agreement between the two legal teams.

11. Marsha Dorgan, "Copple admits guilt in double murder, Napa man enters plea deal, will spend life in prison without the possibility of parole," *The Napa Valley Register*, 9 December 2006.

12. Marsha Dorgan, "Tears, anger, a life in prison," *The Napa Valley Register*, 12 January 2007.

13. Cathy Harrington, "Statement by the Rev. Cathy Harrington," *The San Francisco Gate*, 11 January 2007.

14. Genesis 26:24, Isaiah 43:5. It is interesting how many times throughout the Bible, both God and Jesus tells us "Do not be afraid," and "for I am with you," but how often one forgets these words when needed the most.

15. Avot 2:20 and 2:21.

Chapter 10

Coming Alongside Others: Redemptive Engagement

Harold Heie

Harold Heie is a Senior Fellow at the Center for Christian Studies at Gordon College, Wenham, Massachussets, where he served as Founding Director from 1994 to 2003. He previously served as Vice-President for Academic Affairs at Messiah College (1988-1993) and Northwestern College in Iowa (1980-1988). Before that, he taught mathematics at Gordon College (1975-1980) and The King's College (1963-1975).

Heie has a B.M.E. degree from the Polytechnic University, an M.S.M.E. from the University of Southern California, and an M.A. and Ph.D. in mechanical and aerospace engineering from Princeton University. He has co-authored (with David Wolfe) *Slogans or Distinctives: Reforming Christian Education* (1993), and co-edited *The Reality of Christian Learning: Strategies for Faith-Discipline Integration* (1988, with David Wolfe) and *The Role of Religion in Politics and Society* (1998, with A. James Rudin and Marvin Wilson). He recently authored *Learning to Listen, Ready to Talk: A Pilgrimage Toward Peacemaking* (2007). He has had published a number of essays on the nature of Christian higher education in the *Christian Scholar's Review* and other journals and books. He also serves as a Senior Fellow for the Council for Christian Colleges & Universities (CCCU) and as a Trustee for the Center for Public Justice.

Three premises provide the first element of coherence to this apparently disparate collection of eight case study essays:

- All of God's Creation suffers brokenness because of sin (to paraphrase Rom. 8:19-22, all of God's Creation "groans for redemption").
- The good news of the Christian gospel is that through the person and work of Jesus Christ, God intends to redeem "all of Creation," reconciling humans to God, to each other, and to all aspects of Creation (see Col. 1:15-20).
- All Christians are called to be agents, in partnership with God, for fostering God's redemptive purposes (2 Cor. 5:18-20 suggests that Christians are to be "messengers of reconciliation").

The conviction that God's redemptive purposes extend to *all of Creation* is illustrated (albeit not exhaustively) by these case-study reports of "redemptive engagement" in a wide variety of venues or areas of discourse: environmental practices (Emmerich), film (Hafer), politics (DeWeese), the academy (Waller and Thom), the church (King), criminal justice (Krause), and interfaith dialogue (Wilson). As disparate as these areas are, there is a common mode of engagement intended to be redemptive, a second element of coherence, that Steve Monsma has called "the dialogue model of cultural engagement."

Monsma has proposed three steps in his dialogue model. The substance of these case studies provide marvelous examples of the efficacy of this model and insights into some of their deepest dimensions. I will consider each step in turn.

BUILDING RELATIONSHIPS OF MUTUAL TRUST

The first step Monsma proposes for his "dialogue model of cultural engagement" is "establishing a spirit of mutual trust and respect with those with whom one disagrees." Monsma then proposes that this first step requires that we need to *"get to know* on a personal level those with whom we disagree" (emph. added). Every one of our essayists confirm this need to get to know others as an indispensable step toward building mutual trust.

An excellent example is the stark contrast Susan Emmerich portrays between ways in which the staff of the Chesapeake Bay Foundation (CBF) engaged the watermen of Tangier Island and her own interpersonal strategy. The CBF staff made lifestyle choices that flaunted the cultural values of the watermen of Tangier Island, and they didn't "take the time to understand the Tangiermen's faith worldview nor to speak in terms understood within that worldview." This "led the Tangiermen to be suspicious of the environmentalists' motivations for being on the island and suspicious of their message" (leading to the "mistrust" that Emmerich says "was the single most important cause of the conflict between the Tangier people and the CBF"). In striking contrast, Emmerich's interpersonal strategy included living with the families of the watermen "at the same economic level as the majority of the islanders, to comprehend better their way of life and economic hardships," and socializing with the families of the watermen (even attending their worship services). As a result, she was "developing relationships, trust, and credibility among the faith community."

Jim Waller's mode of engagement with an elite group of Holocaust and Genocide scholars is the most unusual example of the priority of getting to know those you wish to engage. His getting to know these scholars went beyond the formalities of scholarly interaction to informal interpersonal engagement that included talk about children, families, and personal hopes and aspirations for the future (even including Waller's being the "designated driver" for the group of scholars for a night on the town after a long day of scholarly discourse).

Of course, Waller notes that schmoozing is not a good substitute for bad scholarly work. He found, however, that sound scholarly work and taking the time to build relationships of mutual trust with his colleagues was a potent combination as he sought to enable his theory as to why ordinary people sometimes do extraordinary evil—a theory deeply informed by his Christian faith commitment—to gain a fair hearing among scholars who do not share his faith commitment.

As already suggested from Emmerich's experience on Tangier Island, this process of getting to know those you wish to engage requires time. Marv Wilson testifies to this in spades from his forty-five years of interfaith dialogue with the Jewish community. He focuses on the need for Christians to "know [about the other] if they wish to be known [by the other]." Early in his engagement with the Jewish community, he realized that evangelicals and Jews "really did not know each other." They passed like "ships in the night." He concluded that "to know is not to confront abruptly, then dismiss quickly. To know implies a process; it is not 'bump and run,'" and this requires a commitment of time. As Wilson elaborates, "one must be committed to making gradual progress, with small steps rather than quick giant strides. . . . It takes a commitment of time over many months—even years—to come to know the other and to build trust with the other."

The experience of Tammy Krause in engaging the families of murder victims speaks eloquently to the need to develop relationships of mutual trust by getting to know one another. As might be expected, the mothers of two young women who had been murdered in the Napa Valley, who had already been traumatized by the media coverage, were cautious, at best, when they first met over lunch with Krause. A stranger to them, Kraus was actually employed by the defense team for the person convicted of these murders. Krause built mutual trust by "answering the families' questions and listening to their skepticism and concerns" ("listening to the apprehension without an answer or argument"), because of her deep conviction that "people need to be heard and feel valued for what they have to say."

Based on his experience as a Michigan legislator, Paul De-Weese introduces an important aspect of building mutual trust that goes beyond the trust between persons that I have focused on thus far. He notes that "once others came to trust that my highest allegiance was not to my caucus but to promoting human dignity and justice, it enabled the development of partnerships and coalitions committed to a common political agenda." Therefore, as Christians seeking to engage others in our culture, we must go beyond building personal relationships of mutual trust; we must also persuade others of the trustworthiness of the substantive positions we are taking relative to the issues at hand. This suggests that we need to find common ground with those who do not share our particular faith commitment but who may well share certain values because of our common humanity (such as the need to foster human dignity and justice).

DeWeese suggests that we can share certain values "by virtue of all humans being created in God's image."

All the essayists quoted above engaged others through face-to-face interaction. In contrast, Jack Hafer and Michael King report on modes of engagement that focus on conversation by other means: through such media as essays, books, films, paintings, and musical performances. But even here, the need to build relationships of mutual trust is pivotal. The filmmaker Hafer suggests that "the content, tone, and style of the film can build a mutual trust between filmmakers." And he argues persuasively that all Christians should become engaged in the "Great Conversation" about "what makes up the essence of humanity, its great questions and concerns," adding that the Christian church should "encourage youth who want to go into the arts to do so with a sense of high calling, as truth-spreaders."

In a similar vein, Michael King's engagement with the larger culture includes means other than face-to-face conversation, focusing on the written word. In doing so relative to the highly contested debates on homosexuality within the Mennonite community, King raises the provocative question as to which conversation strategy is preferable, face-to-face or written. His own response is that "different conversation strategies fit different circumstances." He suggests that, at times, written conversations may be the best place to start because of "their slower pace and lack of an urgent need for reply," providing those in conversation time to think through what they can learn from those who disagree with them. As one Mennonite denominational leader added, "One reason [the conversation] may have to begin in places like books is that other safe places are often not available."

Finally, Paul DeWeese and David Thom provide a marvelous transition to the second step in the "dialogue model of cultural engagement" proposed by Steve Monsma (after building relationships of mutual trust by getting to know one another): the step of seeking to *understand* the positions of those who disagree with you, including their motivations. DeWeese notes that in his experience as a Michigan legislator, as he got to know the black community, "he began to understand better their experiences." Thom's experience in offering Roundtables to faculty in Amherst and Cambridge is that "you need to get to know people well enough to understand why they believe as they do."

COMING TO UNDERSTAND WHY OTHERS BELIEVE AS THEY DO

The second step that Monsma proposes in his dialogue model is "coming to understand why those who are opposed to us take the positions that we see as being wrong." A crucial factor in coming to understand another person is to gain insight into her "social location," which includes the particularities that define who she is. That is why this second step must be preceded by the "getting to know her" focus of the first step of building mutual trust.

What, then, are the particularites that define who one is? In addition to the characteristics that cannot be missed (like gender and race), these particularities include one's social and economic class, one's personal biography (possibly including pivotal experiences that have shaped a person), and the religious or intellectual traditions in which the person is embedded. Many of these particularities will often have an influence on the position a person takes relative to any topic being discussed. Therefore, to understand adequately the position that a given person may take relative to the issue at hand, it is important to understand the various particularities of that person.

This is why Susan Emmerich calls into question an approach to doing social science that believes "that being detached from the subjects is the only way to achieve an accurate representation of the reality of the situation." She elaborates relative to her own environmental research: "Neither environmental professionals nor academics can hope to solve environmental problems with an approach that simply addresses a particular scientific or technical issue absent the human context in which these issues exist. Public policy professionals and scholars need to generate approaches to environmental problems with and for the people directly involved and within the relational context of peoples' community and culture." Thus her approach to doing an ethnography of the Tangier watermen was to use a "participatory paradigm that allows the researcher to be more interpersonal and relational rather than impersonal and detached." Using this paradigm, she was "giving a voice to others by providing a means for the researcher to discover and understand people's unique history and views about their world."

In addition to seeking an understanding of the Tangier fishermen by listening to them, Emmerich "conducted several months of preliminary research on the regional and communal context in which the watermen live and work and the relationships between watermen and scientists." She "read many books on the history of the Methodist church in the region and its influences, the political and economic history of the region and the islands, and the psychological make-up of fishermen, islanders, and their blood cousins the Appalachian mountain people."

The importance of taking such steps to understand adequately those you wish to engage is the crucial starting point for the gift of hospitality that David Thom has extended to faculty in the Amherst and Cambridge Roundtables devoted to exploring the "intersection of current academic thought and Christian thought." His primary strategy is to provide a welcoming place where scholars can lay bare not only their beliefs on the issue at hand but can share, with those seated around the same table, the experiences and particularities that inform those beliefs. As Thom reports, the non-Christian scholars involved in these roundtables are asking Christian scholars to "start listening to us . . . to try to understand our beliefs," so we can then proceed to the next step of talking about our disagreements.

A marvelous byproduct of this hospitality is that it allows all the Roundtable participants to begin to understand not only the differing beliefs about others but also the experiences and particularities that inform those differing beliefs. That this has proven to be eye-opening to some participants is testified to by two cogent comments from participants: "It was interesting to talk to people whose ideas I had never encountered before and whose perspective I could not necessarily guess right away"; "I was able to hear my own thoughts on the topic articulated by others in novel ways. I was also forced to consider perspectives that did not come naturally to me." It appears that these Roundtables have taken great strides toward helping participants to at least understand one another (a necessary first step before talking about their differences).

This step of enabling persons who disagree on important issues to first understand each other takes giant strides toward ameliorating a pervasive problem when persons disagree—that of stereotyping (or even demonizing) the other. As Marv Wilson's case study report emphasizes, when Jews and Christians do not take the necessary steps to understand each other, we easily resort to stereotyping. To generalize, lack of understanding feeds the temptation to stereotype those who disagree with us. Jim Waller presents a splendid concrete example of how greater understanding can avoid stereotyping, as he reports on his experience with his secular colleagues: "Through their interaction with me, for all my flaws, they at least see that the Christian world is much more diverse and less predictable on the inside than it looks on the outside; that Christians do not all speak (or shout) in one voice."

A fair warning must now be given. When I claim, as I have above, that a person's views on a given issue is informed by her particularities, which we must seek to understand, I am not accepting the stark relativism that holds that since we have differing particularities that may lead to differing views on a given issue, it follows that one view is as adequate as the other. If I believed that, I could terminate this chapter now, for the conversation I hope for then has no point. To fully understand why someone holds a particular view is not to settle the question of whether that view is adequate. To that question I now turn: Assuming we now fully understand each other, how, if at all, can we adjudicate differing views on the issue at hand? This brings us to Monsma's proposed third step in a dialogue model for engaging others.

LEARNING FROM A PERSON WHO DISAGREES WITH YOU

The third step in Monsma's dialogue model for cultural engagement is that of "persons on the other side [of the issue] altering their positions—or, you, perhaps, altering your position—so as to reach greater, even if not, complete agreement." Monsma suggests that this step should begin with trying to find some "common ground" (noting that such an "area of agreement" may be having similar "goals," with the differing views focusing on "the means to reach those goals"). A good example of success in finding some common ground is provided in Susan Emmerich's observation that "the common goal bridging the gap

184 / Mutual Treasure

between the watermen and CBF was a mutual value—the desire for clean islands and a healthy Chesapeake Bay fishery."

But, once some initial common ground is found, how do you navigate the differences that remain? Is there a way to talk about the remaining differences in a manner that leads to mutual learning that ameliorates some of the initial differences, leading down the road to more common ground? To that most difficult question, I now turn, drawing on the meaning of "genuine conversation" proposed by Michael King.

King summarizes his view of "genuine conversation" as "involving a mutual quest for treasures in our own and the other's viewpoint. The first move is 'to make as clear as I can why I hold this position . . . and why you might find in it treasure to value in you own quest for truth.' The second move is 'to see the value in the other's view . . . and to grow in my own understandings by incorporating as much of the other's perspective as I can without losing the integrity of my own convictions.'"[1] The ideal is that those in conversation view themselves as "partners in a quest for understandings larger than any alone could find." King's own extensive experiences with such genuine conversations led him to observe that he was "drawn to the growing conviction that any perspective has treasure to offer."

In my own words, this compelling view of the meaning of "genuine conversation," which I take to be the heart of the dialogue model for engagement, means that in my dialogue with another person about a set of initial differences that she and I may have on a given issue, we both try to understand each other well enough to identify the best in each other's insights. We are then open to the possibility of modifying our original positions based on the insights of the other, in a way that actually enriches each of our original positions.

Is there evidence of such "mutual learning" having taken place in our various case studies, and if so, has such mutual learning been helped by careful attention having first been paid to the first two steps in Monsma's model: building relationships of mutual trust; and coming to understand why other believe as they do? Yes! Let me mention just three illustrations.

Witness two testimonies from Paul DeWeese: "I frequently worked alongside African-American clergy in Lansing. . . . I began to worship with their congregations on Sundays. . . . As I listened, *I began to understand better the ways in which I benefited from 'white privilege'"* (emph. added); "I had worked hard to develop personal relationships with legislators from the Democratic Party. This evolved over time into honest discussions regarding particular bills. These discussions often enabled me to ask questions I hadn't previously thought to ask, and *to gain perspectives I previously lacked"* (emph. added). While these two testimonies are limited to what DeWeese learned from the African-American community through genuine conversation, he also implies that fourteen influential black pastors in Lansing had learned enough about his "commitment to racial reconciliation" to call a press conference to support his candidacy for the State Senate.

The case of Jim Waller also testifies to the accomplishment of mutual learning built on building relationships of mutual trust and understanding the other. First, he learned from his friendship-based conversations with his "secular" colleagues that "an increasing number of them wouldn't even describe themselves as 'secular'—forcing [him] to reexamine [his] assumptions about the validity of 'secular' as a descriptor." At the same time, his engagement with these other scholars led them to question "their homogeneous stereotypes of all Christians as 'anti-intellectual,' 'evangelical,' 'fundamentalist,' or 'conservative,'" adding that "through their interaction with me, for all my flaws, they at least see that the Christian world is much more diverse and less predictable on the inside than it looks on the outside."

Particularly revealing to his colleagues was Waller's "willingness to engage in self-critique" in relation to religion's "role in genocide" by "beating . . . colleagues to the punch in criticizing religion." Waller reports that his willingness to be self-critical in this way opened the door for his being able to make "the case for religion in the human experience." These examples from Waller bear eloquent testimony to his experience that "engagement with ideas is, of necessity, engagement with others (real people) who carry those ideas."

The Emmerich case provides another good example of genuine conversation leading to mutual learning. Although she does not provide us with the details of what the Tangiermen and the CBF staff learned from each other, significant learning about one another obviously took place for their interaction "led to individual Tangiermen asking forgiveness from CBF staff for ostracizing them and to CBF staff asking for forgiveness for their mistakes."

If you are now thinking that all of the above "sounds too good to be *always* true," you are correct. For the experience of Michael King suggests that the ideal quest for mutual learning through genuine conversation that he so eloquently describes may be unattainable when the topic being discussed is as controversial as homosexuality. To this concern and another possible "limitation" on the ideal quest for genuine conversation I now turn.

LIMITATIONS ON THE QUEST FOR GENUINE CONVERSATION

The ideal of having "genuine conversation," as defined by King, may be unattainable in certain situations, for two reasons: the tendency for humans to limit their categories of thought to "binary opposites" (e. g., bad/good, right/wrong, righteous/evil); and the problem of "power differentials" between those engaging one another. I will consider these limitations in turn.

Thinking Only in Terms of Binary Opposites

King laments that when human beings discuss extremely contentious issues, like homosexuality, they seem more attracted to "battle" than to the ideal of "mutual learning" that is the crux of his definition of genuine conversation. He speaks from experience: "After spending decades pursuing alternatives to battling over homosexuality, I see no overwhelming evidence that such a vision [for genuine conversation resulting in mutual learning] will carry the day." In commenting on the contributors to his *Dreamseeker Magazine* issue on homosexuality, he notes that "its writers tended to persist in seeing each other as combatants rather than partners in a quest for understanding larger than any alone could find."

Why is that? King says this reflects the propensity of humans to limit their categories of thought to "binary opposites": "It remains unclear to me whether humans, in general or Christian, are capable of sustained 'genuine' conversation as opposed to seeing life as made up of binaries [bad/good, right/wrong, curse/gift, all nature/all nurture], one of which we champion, the other of which we aim to defeat."

Both Steve Monsma and Marv Wilson echo this concern expressed by King. Monsma notes that one of the characteristics of those who take a "confrontational" approach to engaging others is their conviction that "they have the answer and their attitude is, 'I know I am right and you are wrong, so take it or leave it, but don't expect me to meet you halfway or seek to understand why you believe as you do'."

Marv Wilson notes that one of the obstacles to the interfaith dialogue between evangelicals and Jews he champions is that evangelicals do not realize sufficiently that "they may often have to be satisfied with *incomplete answers* and *partial agreement* on various interfaith discussion points" (emph. added). If one thinks in terms of the binary opposites of either being right (completely) or wrong (completely), the idea of settling for "partial agreement" (based on the treasures uncovered in each other's perspectives, to use King's terminology) is anathema.

How, then does one counteract this apparent tendency for humans to resist genuine conversation because of thinking in binary opposites? I have two suggestions. The first is to remind all humans, Christian or otherwise, that none of us is God (or some other all-knowing being). To believe that on complex, highly controversial issues, you are completely right and the other is completely wrong reflects hubris disconnected from the fact that to be human entails being finite and fallible. Such hubris needs to be replaced by a healthy dose of humility—a precondition for genuine conversation to which I will return later.

My second response draws on a proposal for an attenuated view of "what makes a conversation genuine" proposed by Carolyn Schrock-Shenk in the foreword to the book on homosexuality King edited. She asks "What makes dialogue genuine?" Her surprising and provocative response: "Does one need to be open to changing one's perspective or conviction about an issue? In my view, that readiness is the ideal, but it is rarely realistic, especially in relation to issues as charged as homosexuality. I have come to believe that *a minimum requirement for genuine conversation* [emph. added] is a readiness to change or modify one's perspective about *the person or persons* [her italics] holding the opposite point of view."[2]

Note carefully what Schrock-Shenk is suggesting. The "ideal" is still the "genuine conversation" King (and all the other contributors to this volume) hope for: that through conversation, persons would be open to refining their perspectives on the issue at hand in light of the treasures they discover in the perspectives of others. But, given the current state of the raging debate among Christians regarding homosexuality, that ideal may be unrealistic at this time.

However, it is no small thing if, at a minimum, those taking opposing sides in this debate at least modify their perspectives on those who disagree with them as a result of dialogue. To be more specific, those Christians taking opposite sides on this volatile issue may come to see that those on the other side are also deeply committed Christians, with whom they can have fellowship despite disagreements about homosexuality. Attaining that sort of "unity in fellowship" (not uniformity in beliefs about homosexuality) would be no small accomplishment in those Christian denominations that threaten to split over the homosexuality issue.

I can attest to the wisdom in Schrock-Shenk's suggestion based on my participation in an eight-hour "Dialogue on Homosexuality" sponsored by my own denomination, the Reformed Church in America (RCA), hosted at my home church, the American Reformed Church in Orange City, Iowa. As part of the dialogue, the leader paired up each attendee with another person for one-on-one conversation. I was paired with a local minister whom I didn't know but who had a reputation for taking a strong, even strident position on homosexuality with which I would disagree.

I thoroughly enjoyed our time together. We got to know one another, talking first about family, including our discovery that we had both lived in New Jersey in the past (later in the session, he introduced his two daughters to me, fine Christian women attending a college in Pennsylvania). We had differing views on homosexuality. Although we didn't have much time together, I think we came to understand each other better.

I don't think our conversation changed our contrasting views. Nevertheless, I came away from the session believing that I had come to know a good, deeply committed Christian. Even though I disagreed with him about this contentious issue, I felt we could still fellowship together within the RCA denomination based on our common commitment to Jesus Christ. I hope he came away from our conversation with the same feeling.

The Problem of Power Differentials

To present this problem in stark terms, consider the following excerpt form a recent book on "How to Talk About Hot Topics on Campus"[3] by means of what the authors call "moral conversation" (which bears some similarities to what Michael King has called "genuine conversation" but also some differences):

> One of the authors . . . remembers a black student activist once saying to him that she found it impossible to relate to his notion of moral conversation because it was too white and too middle class. For her, the "civility movement" is "hung up" on a politics of politeness; thus it completely misses the need to attack at their source the basic social problems that plague America. Moral conversation, in her view, implies a kindness and empathy among opponents trying to understand each other's perspective that is unrealistic in the face of tangible oppression and cruelty. Moral conversation is another example of the naiveté implicit in white privilege, she said, because often the only way that Black Americans and other oppressed minorities can get heard is when they raise their voices in anger.
>
> There are times, she said, that the enemy does indeed need to be demonized. . . . To the activist left, moral conversation is nothing more than a tool of those entrenched in power, and this is the group that sets the terms of civil dialogue. (pp. 31-32)

This statement must be taken with the utmost seriousness. It is certainly true that when there is a significant power differential between persons in conversation, easy talk about engaging in genuine conversation is ludicrous. Two responses come to mind. The first is to point to some examples (from our essayists) in which those in positions of power have voluntarily relinquished their power to create an even playing field where genuine conversation can occur. The second is to consider the possibility, as Steve Monsma has suggested, that there may be situations where "confrontation" is called for.

The Powerful Coming Alongside the Powerless

Paul DeWeese suggests that "the first temptation [for the Christian politician] is the *seduction of power*." His story indicates, however, that he did not succumb to that temptation. Rather, he consistently worked as an advocate on behalf of the relatively powerless in his legislative district, the African-American community whose needs were not being addressed adequately by most politicians wielding political power. He notes that he "frequently worked *alongside* the African-American community" (emph. added). Such coming alongside involved drawing "close enough to . . . persons [in dire need] to be able to 'feel their pain'."

DeWeese also was an advocate on behalf of the Michigan State workers. He initiated a State Worker Appreciation Day to honor state workers who had become marginalized because they worked for a government viewed by the general citizenry as unproductive. State workers flocked to these events because they were "eager to hear someone honor their hard work."

Tammy Krause also was a powerful advocate on behalf of relatively powerless families of victims of murder. As Krause notes, the powerlessness that the families of victims experience is inherent in the adversarial nature of our criminal justice system: "Both sides of the legal fence view victims as an entity that needs to be controlled throughout the duration of the case to ensure their side's strategy wins. This is often due to the adversarial nature of the legal system in which one side must always have something 'over' the other side to win a case."

Even though she was employed by the defense lawyers for the accused murderer, she (with their blessing) came *alongside* the families of the families of the victims, making herself "vulnerable" and being "present to the unfolding of . . . [their] pain and struggle," thereby being an advocate for these families to "have a voice" in the criminal proceedings. She beautifully describes the joy that results when these families "find their voice" as follows: "When you journey alongside persons faithfully and witness their dark moments of pain and suffering, there will be a time that you are present when they find their voice and they sing the song which never stops and you know you are in a very holy place."

Susan Emmerich also came *alongside* the relatively powerless Tangier watermen in their conflict with the CBF staff. In her own words, she was an "encourager, educator . . . , and peace-maker who legitimized, sustained, and advocated" on behalf of the watermen, adding that central to these responsibilities was the role of a *"paraclete,"* the Greek translation of which is "called alongside of." As Emmerich said, "'I walked alongside of' the people for a time."

Emmerich adds that in her role as "advocate" she "not only legitimizes and sustains the challenge of the weaker party [the watermen] but also speaks openly with and for the weaker party, helping them to identify resources and articulate needs. I advocated and worked to legitimate the involvement of the Tangier women and disenfranchised Tangier watermen in the fishery regulation discussion and decision making." Not everyone took kindly to her advocacy on the part of the weaker party, for she received some "death threats" and "ostracization from certain community members."

On careful reading, it can be seen that all of our case study reports (not just the three dramatic ones noted above) exemplify Christians engaging others in our culture by coming alongside of them, getting to know them enough to understand them, as a prelude to engaging them in genuine conversation.[4] In this light, the message of our book to those Christians who are in situations in which power differentials make genuine conversation impossible is that Christians are called (as agents of God's redemptive purposes) to come alongside the powerless, advocating for their needs and for them to have a voice as a necessary condition for the possibility of genuine conversation.

What if, however, such advocacy on behalf of the powerless fails? What if the powerful keep the powerless "in their place?" As suggested by the black student activist quoted above, is the only remaining resort "confrontation?" To these difficult questions I now turn.

Confrontation as a Last Resort?

As you will recall, Steve Monsma draws on the way in which Jesus engaged the Pharisees, as recorded in Matthew 23, to suggest that confrontation may be appropriate in unusual situations, at least for Christians engaging other Christians, when three conditions are met: "when the persons being confronted already have an accurate understanding of the Christian truth, have persistently rejected it, and are in positions of leadership where they are leading many others astray."

I must confess that I do not possess sufficient wisdom to know what to make of this example of how Jesus engaged the hypocritical Pharisees to offer any generalization for the behavior of others, Christian or otherwise, as to whether confrontation is ever called for. I can only answer for myself. Confrontation is inimical to my understanding of the call of Jesus for me to love others (more about that shortly). Therefore, if I found myself in a situation in which confrontation appeared to be called for (as when the powerful are decimating the weak), I hope that I would, by God's grace, commit myself to active advocacy on behalf of the weak (whatever the consequences for me), but in a manner that opened up the possibility for genuine conversation (as in the situations in which DeWeese, Krause, and Emmerich found themselves).

PRECONDITIONS FOR GENUINE CONVERSATION

The dialogic model for Christians to engage culture, focusing on the need for genuine conversation, presupposes that Christians will exemplify some cardinal Christian virtues: humility, patience, and love.

Humility

Jack Hafer reminds us of the biblical teaching that "we see in a mirror, dimly" (1 Cor. 13:12). For Marv Wilson, this teaching means that Christians need to be reminded that we "presently know only 'in part'." We do not have a "God's-eye view" of the Truth. This speaks of the need for humility as we present our finite, fallible understandings of the "truth" relative to the issue at hand when we engage in genuine conversation with those who may disagree with us. The story told by Jim Waller is a marvelous example of expressing three forms of such humility—worldview, intellectual, and relational—in his engagement with secular colleagues in Holocaust and Genocide Studies.

It is all too easy to mistake such humility for stark relativism: you have your truth claims, I have mine; end of conversation. But that is a glaring mistake. Exercising humility does not mean that you discard your own understanding of the truth or believe that any one understanding is as good as any other. You present your own understanding of the truth, with conviction, in genuine conversation—but in openness to (or better, active exploration of) the possibility that as a finite, fallible human being, your understanding may not be adequate and you can refine or correct your understanding through genuine conversation with others. As Waller puts it, "I hold my faith with *sufficient certainty,* but not with *absolute certainty."*

Ian Barbour has put the same idea in a different way in his definition of "religious maturity": "It is by no means easy to hold beliefs for which you would be willing to die, and yet to remain open to new insights; but it is precisely such a combination of commitment and inquiry that constitutes religious maturity."[5] Barbour is pointing to a very rare combination that must be held in tension, both commitment and openness. At one pole, commitment, without openness, too easily leads to fanaticism, even terrorism. At the other extreme, openness, without any commitment, too easily leads to stark relativism. Christians wishing to engage in genuine conversation must evidence both commitment and openness.

One of the participants in a Roundtable hosted by David Thom gave eloquent testimony to the way in which the renowned Christian scholar John Polkinghorne expressed both commitment and openness in his conversation with a mixed audience of Christian and secular scholars:

> The speaker [Polkinghorne] . . . has a wonderful hospitality. By that I mean something far beyond politeness or graciousness. Rather, in his arguing for his own views and explanation as to why he does not hold certain alternative views he never puts anyone else down. Quite the reverse: he creates safe space for real encounter between people of differing views.

Such hospitality requires a willingness to listen well. Marv Wilson suggests that such "listening" may be the "ultimate form of humility." And, as David Thom suggests in recounting the experience of Kelly Monroe Kullberg when faced with a hostile audience at a major state university, "the very act of listening can disarm those who come to the table intent on not listening to anything you may want to say."

Patience

Many Christians, especially those with an evangelical bent, have a propensity to want quick answers to complex issues or problems. As already noted, Marv Wilson lays that desire to rest in his report on forty-five years of genuine conversations with his Jewish friends as they seek to better understand each other in their respective quests for truth. As Wilson states, "Inaccuracies and misperceptions of the other cannot be overcome overnight." Wilson has demonstrated a great measure of patience, which, in my own words, is based on "the hope that though ongoing respectful conversations, greater understanding will gradually emerge as a gift."[6]

Chris K. Huebner beautifully captures the essence of such patience in his observations about the "nonviolent epistemology" of the late distinguished Mennonite theologian John Howard Yoder. Huebner suggests that "theology operates according to a violent logic of speed whenever it is unwilling to risk the possibility that truthfulness is the outcome of ongoing, timeful, 'open conversation'."[7] In contrast "Yoder's nonviolent epistemology . . . assumes that truthfulness is an utterly contingent gift that can only be given and received and that it emerges at the site of vulnerable interchange with the other."[8] We must overcome our propensity to want quick answers to complex questions.

Marv Wilson notes that the biblical admonition to exercise patience is based on an even more foundational Christian virtue, that of love: "Love is patient . . . [and] endures all things" (1 Cor. 13:4, 7).

Love

There is no ambiguity in Jesus' call for Christians to love others (Matt. 22: 34-40). As Marv Wilson elaborates, "'Love your neighbor as yourself' is a pivotal command incumbent on all Christians. Moses established this teaching, and Jesus re-enforced it, declaring that love of God and neighbor is the mega-commandment for his followers (Lev. 19:18; Mark 12:28-34)." Wilson adds, "Is it not presumptuous for a Christian to claim he 'loves his neighbors' when he has made little effort to know and understand those of different faith traditions living in his locale?"

But, what does the command to love others have to do with the call to engage others in genuine conversation? To me, everything! It is a deep expression of my love for another when I create a welcoming space for her to express disagreement, when I take the trouble to get to know her sufficiently to understand her position by empathetically putting myself in her shoes, and when I seek treasures in her point of view, hoping that she also finds treasures in my point of view. My commitment to fostering such genuine conversation is not peripheral to my Christian faith. It is a central expression of my faith, in grateful response to Jesus' love for me and his call for me to love others.

But, how far should we take this call to love others? Michael King challenges us to take it to the limit, noting that "the heartbeat" of his approach is "Jesus' teaching to love enemies." In his own words, King says, "maybe if Jesus taught us to love rather than kill human enemies, he would want us to love rather than kill our prejudice or viewpoint 'enemies.' And how do you love an enemy viewpoint without somehow learning from it, or at least respecting it, at least looking for nuggets of treasure in it even if you in the end persist in seeing much greater treasure in your own stand?"

When I view television interviews with some well-known evangelical leaders of our day (which, frankly, I try to avoid), I am saddened by the lack of humility, patience, and love of others in their pronouncements. The general public would gain a more balanced view of how Christians wish to engage others if the media would interview some of our essayists. They are my contemporary Christian heroes.

A CONCLUDING CHALLENGE

At the same time that Michael King bemoans the prevalence of thinking in terms of binary opposites that often seem to decimate the possibility of engaging others in genuine conversation, he insightfully suggests that he too may have fallen into binary thinking. In his own words, "perhaps I need to break also out of the binary Carry the Day/Not Carry the Day." Every effort at orchestrating genuine conversation will hopefully lead to some mutual learning, but, as King's extensive experience suggests, there will also be many disappointments.

How should one respond to such disappointment? King urges us to view them as "seeds," observing that "such disappointments seemed to be the seeds of a next step. If this was an effort at genuine conversation rather than combat, then fallibilities of one effort and the criticisms rightly highlighting them should be treated not as occasions for battle but opportunities to keep pursuing conversation." King adds, "Is this [fostering genuine conversation] the seed God has called a few of us to plant in the world, wherever and however it may take root. . . ?"

I like that, because the primary way I have come to view my own labors over the years is that I have been planting "seeds of redemption" (see Matt. 13:31-32), entrusting the harvest into God's hands. This means that those of us committed to the dialogue model for engaging others in our culture, focusing on orchestrating genuine conversation, need to just keep on planting seeds. This need to "keep on keeping on," as they say, is captured beautifully in the following closing quotes from Michael King and Tammy Krause:

"Maybe my job, our job, is not mainly to win, even when the quest is to stop dividing the world into Winners/Losers, My Prejudice Good/Your Prejudice Bad. Maybe our job is to plant, and God's job is to harvest. But whatever God harvests, I hope over time it will lead to fewer enemies and more brothers and sisters" (King).

"I remember the words of the Talmud that resonate in me, 'You are not required to complete the task, yet you are not free to withdraw from it.' When my work on a case is complete, I send up a prayer of gratitude for experiencing holiness in such unexpected places and another for the light that hope brings" (Krause).

NOTES

1. Michael A. King, ed., *Stumbling Toward a Genuine Conversation on Homosexuality* (Telford, Pa.: Cascadia Publishing House, 2007), p. 26

2. King, p. 15.

3. Robert J. Nash, DeMethra LaSha Bradley, Arthur W. Chickering, *How to Talk About Hot Topics on Campus: From Polarization to Moral Conversation.* (San Francisco: Jossey-Bass, 2008).

4. The story of my own pilgrimage toward a focus on orchestrating forums for genuine conversation is told in Harold Heie, *Learning to Lis-*

ten, Ready to Talk: A Pilgrimage Toward Peacemaking (New York: iUniverse, 2007). I like to think that this present book is a natural sequel to my 2007 book in the sense that my earlier account lays the foundation for the project I directed at the Center for Christian Studies at Gordon College that eventually led to the emergence of this collection of essays.

5. Ian Barbour, *Myths, Models, and Paradigms: A Comparative Study in Science and Religion.* New York: Harper & Row, 1974), p. 138.

6. Heie, p. 92.

7. Chris K. Huebner, "Patience, Witness, and the Scattered Body of Christ: Yoder and Virilio on Knowledge, Politics, and Speed," in *A Mind Patient and Untamed: Assessing John Howard Yoder's Contribution to Theology, Ethics, and Peacemaking,* ed. Ben C. Ollenberger and Gayle Gerber Koontz (Telford, Pa.: Cascadia Publishing House, 2004), p. 67

8. Huebner, p. 66.

The Index

www.ingramcontent.com/pod-product-compliance
Lightning Source LLC
Chambersburg PA
CBHW031509270326
41930CB00006B/324